CPE

Character, Plot, & Emotion

The Three Foundational Pillars of Storytelling

Diana Stout, MFA, Ph.D.

Copyright © 2024 Diana Stout, MFA, PhD

All rights reserved.

No part of this book may be reproduced or transmitted in any form or by any means without prior written permission from the author, except as permitted by U.S. copyright law.

Michael Hauge's material used with permission.

All other graphics, charts, and illustrations are the creation of the author and cannot be replicated or used in any document or publication, including social media without the author's permission.

Cover design by
Sharpened Pencils Productions LLC

ISBN: 979-8-9870751-4-2

"With *CPE: Character, Plot and Emotion*, Diana Stout brilliantly reveals and edifies the uniquely powerful principles of plot and character created by eight writers and consultants who are regarded as masters of storytelling for film and fiction. But the real treasure of this wonderful book is how she simplifies and combines their methods with her own expertise as a hugely accomplished novelist, teacher, and consultant. The result (along with its accompanying workbook) is an essential guide to transforming the emotional impact and commercial success of your own storytelling."

Michael Hauge, author of *Writing Screenplays That Sell, Selling Your Story in 60 Seconds, The Hero's Two Journeys* (with Christopher Vogler), and *Storytelling Made Easy* (for business leaders, speakers, and entrepreneurs)

DEDICATION

For the writers who struggle and would like an easier time in developing their characters and storylines.

CONTENTS

Acknowledgements xi
CPE 15
  The Three Foundational Pillars of Storytelling 15
Chapter 1 – Laying the Foundation, Part 1 17
  What This Book Contains 18
  How This Book Can Help You 19
  How To Use This Book 20
Chapter 2 – FAQ, Part I 21
Chapter 3 – Laying the Foundation, Part II 27
  And So, The Journey Began 27
  Pantser, Plotter Definitions 28
  Clearing Up the Myths 28
  What the Beta Testers Said 29
Chapter 4 – Laying the Foundation, Part III 35
  Journeying Toward the Masters 35
  Expert Encounters 38
  The Masters 40
    Aristotle 40
    Syd Field 40
    Joseph Campbell 40
    Michael Hauge 41
    Christopher Vogler 42
    John Truby 43
    Blake Snyder 44
    Allen Palmer 45
  Figure 1: Comparison of Experts Chart 47
  CPE Plot Points 48
Chapter 5 – Laying the Foundation, Part IV 49
  Backstory 49

Ghost Event / Ghost Person	50
Ghost Triggers	53
Key Question	54
Magic of Three (3)	55
Why Today?	58
Prologue	58

Chapter 6 – Character 61
Ordinary / Extraordinary	61
BMOC	64
Character Arcs	65
Other Primary Characters	67
Figure 2: Hauge 1988 motivation & character chart	68
The Hero (Protagonist)	69
The Nemesis (Antagonist / True Villian)	71
The Reflection / Buddy (Mentor)	72
Romance (Love Interest, (Fake) Antagonist)	74

Chapter 7 – Plot 77
Mitchell German	77
Figure 3: Story A & B	78
Why We Buy Books and Movie Tickets	79

Chapter 8 – Emotion 81
Emotion as Story's Beating Heart	81
An Exercise Worth Trying	82

Chapter 9 – The Plot Points 85
CPE Plot Points	85
Act I	86
Ordinary World	86
Throwaway Line	89
New Opportunity (10%)	91
Discussion & Decision	91
Meeting the Mentor	92

Act II – Part I 92
  Change of Plans (25%) 92
  Tests, Allies, Enemies 93
  Pinch Point (37%) 94
Act II – Part II 95
  Midpoint Self-Reflection (50%) 95
  First Battle 97
  Pinch Point (62%) 98
  Celebration (False Win) 98
Act III 99
  Major Setback Where All is Lost (75%) 99
  Climax (90-99%) 99
  Claiming the Prize 101
Chapter 10 – The Worksheets 103
  Tools Required 103
    Figure 4: Diana's Science Board Storyboard 103
  How to Recreate the Worksheets 104
  Post-it Note Directions 104
  Creating a Bare Bones Outline 105
    Worksheet 1: Plotting Points 1-6 107
    Worksheet 2: Plotting Points 7-12 109
    Worksheet 3: Plotting Points 13-18 111
    Worksheet 4: Plotting Points 19-24 113
    Worksheet 5: Plotting Points 25-30 115
  Character Worksheets 116
    Worksheet 6: Huuge 1988 motivation & character chart 117
    Worksheet 7: Putting a Square Peg into a Round World 118
  Protagonist Worksheet 119
    Figure 5: Character Square 119

Nemesis / True Villian Worksheet 121
Buddy / Reflection / Mentor Worksheet 121
Love Interest / (Fake) Antagonist Worksheet ... 122
Chapter 11 - My Plotting Process 123
   Step 1: Writing Character Journals 123
   Step 2: Filling in the Character Squares 125
      Figure 6: CCC character squares 127
   Step 3: Filling in Hauge's Character Chart 128
      Figure 7: Hauge's Character Chart for CCC ... 129
   Step 4: Creating Post-its 130
   Step 5: Identifying the 5 Key Plot Points 131
   Step 6: Organizing Scenes 132
      Figure 8: File Folder Plotting 133
      Figure 9: Science Board as Storyboard 134
   Step 7: Starting the Story 134
   Step 8: Editing 137
Chapter 12 – FAQ, Part II 138
      Figure 10: Diana's Plotting Points 1-6 142
      Figure 11: Diana's Plotting Points 7-12 143
      Figure 12: Diana's Plotting Points 13-18 144
      Figure 13: Diana's Plotting Points 19-24 145
      Figure 14: Diana's Plotting Points 25-30 146
Recommended Reading 147
About the Author 149
Also by Diana Stout 150
Follow Diana Stout 151
Can You Help? 152

ACKNOWLEDGEMENTS

Thank you to my beta testers, Lenore, the two Lindas, and the other Diana who took my initial plotting sheets and various revisions of them, and tried them out, giving me excellent feedback in return.

To my beta readers Lenore, the two Lindas, and Anne. I couldn't publish any book without you. Thank you.

And, a standing ovation to the three professionals — writers, screenwriters, producers — who by sharing their discoveries changed my plotting and storytelling abilities forever, providing me with huge, delightful *aha moments:* Christopher Vogler, Michael Hauge, and Allen Palmer.

May my shared journey here bring forth a multitude of *aha moments* for you, just as theirs did for me.

Author's Note

Hero represents both genders when used.

The use of *they* is a singular *they* in most instances, and which has become a grammatical substitution for *him or her, he or she.*

This grammatical style change has taken place in the last few years.

CPE

Character, Plot, & Emotion

The Three Foundational Pillars of Storytelling

Plot is how we become interested in reading the book or seeing the movie. The storyline intrigues us.

Character is how we become engaged in a story. The protagonist is likeable, like us in some way, or is someone we'd like to become. We can relate to their situation or are fascinated by their situation and wish it would happen or hope it never happens to us.

Emotion is the magic ingredient that connects us to both character and plot. If the book or movie can make us gasp, cry, laugh, sit on the edge of our seats, or sigh, it's a story we'll tell others about. We're passionate about sharing emotional experiences. It's why we have so many traditions and celebrations of holidays, weddings, reunions, and other gatherings.

CHAPTER 1 – LAYING THE FOUNDATION, PART 1

Do you struggle with the sagging middle?

Do you get stuck in your writing, not sure where to go in the story?

Have you ever been told your characters are flat, one-dimensional, or unlikable?

Have you ever become bored with your own story?

Have you ever started writing an idea, then shelved it because you didn't know how to finish it?

Have you ever wished you could write faster?

*****

At the beginning of my writing fiction, I was that person.

At first, I didn't understand the monstrous importance that each element of character, plot, and emotion held.

Nor did I understand how important it was for me to find *my* writing process—and not follow someone else's process—so that I would never again find myself stuck.

What This Book Contains

This book is a reference guide, a workbook, and a bit of a memoir as it represents *my writing journey of discovery* and includes what I've taught in my writing classes both inseat and online, in academic and non-academic classrooms, and what I've shared with writers in coaching sessions and presentations.

The Laying the Foundation chapters serve as a reference guide and contain various elements, explanations, examples, and other foundational information.

The FAQ chapters replicate questions I'm frequently asked, and which I split into two chapters—one immediately to address questions you already have. The last FAQ chapter uses terminology you won't know or understand until you read this book, *but* it's an important chapter because it addresses my plotting method based on genre.

Laying the Foundation, Part III is about the masters I encountered on my writing journey. These masters were incredibly important to my learning.

By sharing what I discovered and learned, maybe you'll find a few masters you haven't heard of or investigated yet. Hopefully, they can help you in your journey as they did mine.

The Character, Plot, and Emotion chapters spotlight the importance of each element as a singular element.

The Plot Points chapter spotlights how each plot point pillar blends these three elements of character, plot, and emotion into a page-turning story.

The workbook section replicates the plotting worksheets I produced to help me visualize my story on paper or on a portable storyboard, which could be a file folder or a two-fold science board, both using only one other tool: Post-it notes. The Post-it note size depends on the paper, file, or board that I use.

Directions on how to create these simple worksheets are included, with further directions for each square. However, if you want worksheets you can easily scan or copy, then you may want to purchase this book's companion workbook, the *CPE Workbook*.

Chapter 11 describes my fiction writing process and is filled with how-to details, including a copy of my worksheets that I used to create my historical gothic novelette, *Harbor House: Say You Will*.

How This Book Can Help You

Overall, this book demonstrates how using structural plot points can create the page-turning tension and Deep POV characters that agents, publishers, and producers want and that readers seek.

By no means is this book the end all of plotting and of

creating characters. There are many other writers sharing their process and expertise, as well.

How To Use This Book

Use what works for *your* process, but don't be afraid to experiment, to try something new. You never know what you'll discover when you move out of your comfort zone or long-held habits.

I highly suggest reading the entire book first, so that you fully...

- understand the terminology being used with the worksheets,
- understand how character, plot, and emotion operate both separately *and* with each other,
- eliminate frustrations should you want to jump straight to the worksheets.

That said, feel free to skip early chapters you find overwhelming or confusing at first.

Come back to them later when you have more understanding and want more explanations regarding the masters or specific plot points so you can use the worksheets better.

Use and do what works for *you*!

CHAPTER 2 – FAQ, PART I
(Frequently Asked Questions)

Putting a FAQ at the end of a book is commonplace. I decided to split my FAQ chapter into two parts, with Part I placed among the Laying the Foundation chapters.

Why? Because I know you already have questions!

FAQ, Part I addresses questions I'm frequently asked at the beginning of a consultation. Questions that will aid you in understanding *why* I've provided the resource information before the real reward of this book—the plotting worksheets and their how-to use information.

FAQ, Part II addresses those questions pertaining to using the worksheets with various genres.

Not all genres use the structural pillars the same. Some genres use all of them deeply, other genres use them sparingly.

By the time you finish reading this FAQ chapter, you may be better able to pick and choose which chapters will best apply to the genre(s) you write.

So, here we go...

The questions are posed as if you the readers and writers are asking the questions.

What are the advantages of plotting?

Major holes get revealed *early*.

In my earlier years of writing fiction, I had to remove pages of scenes because fixing the holes changed the dynamics of the story or the characters, rendering previously written pages useless. I was rearranging pages and pages of text.

Now, I'm fixing holes before the first draft occurs. I'm saving time by not having to move or cut scenes as frequently. Thus, I get to start close editing sooner, which includes layering development.

But, if I plot, I'll never be surprised!

My experience has proven that statement to be a falsehood.

While I know the ending and various events that occur along the way, I'm always surprised while writing the scenes.

Even though I know my character's deepest, darkest secret—their wound—they can and do surprise me by what they say or by how they respond.

How long does it take you to plot your books?

For a nonfiction book, it's usually a few days to a week. For fiction, I can spend a few days developing the characters, and then a month plotting out the entire book.

An entire month?

Yes, but I'm creating a lengthy document, one that saves me time in writing the first draft, which may only take one or two months to produce. Plus, the outline material gets integrated into the draft, so none of its content is wasted material; it just gets rewritten.

The following drafts are about revising sentences, choosing better words, polishing the grammar and punctuation, and then finally, publishing the book.

It's one of my secrets to writing fast. Produce a full treatment or story first, then write the script or book as quickly as possible.

Your process may have you plotting for only a few days. Your process will not be the same as mine.

I have yet to find two writers who share the same process.

For someone who has never plotted before, what is your recommendation? Where should I start?

After reading this book, start with the five big plot-turning points of:

- New Opportunity (10%)
- Change of Plans (25%) – start of Act II, Part 1
- Midpoint (50%) – start of Act II, Part 2
- Major Setback (75%) – start of Act III
- Climax (90-99%)

Using the plotting worksheets I explain in Chapter 10, place these five plot points as Post-its on the sheets. Just focus on those five for now and nothing else.

Do they make sense? Do the events during those plot points feel right? Is the action and emotion ratcheted to where you can feel the character's anxiety?

That's the emotion you want to feel when as you develop your story, because if you're not feeling it, your reader won't feel it either.

By performing that one action of putting those five major plot points in position, you'll suddenly have scene ideas gushing forth like a spigot turned on.

I've watched it happen to writers who perform this activity for the first time. Their excitement is contagious.

Go with the new experience! See, if you don't become more passionate about the story by getting these plot points out of your head and on paper. Doing so creates an open stream where ideas can flow forth easily.

Often, we don't realize how we dam up our ideas by not getting them out of our head.

What will I lose by going directly to the worksheet chapters first?

Let me respond with a metaphor, giving you a visual.

Let's say you want to build a house, but you want to save time, so you scrape the earth level, and put in your corner posts so you can build your walls.

The walls go up quickly, and you put up a roof. Then, you finally lay the floors—tile, wood, or carpet. On the dirt.

In your desire to move in quickly, you skipped laying the foundation: the cement that will keep the walls anchored and straight and a barrier between your floors and the bare ground.

These first few following chapters are the equivalent of that cement foundation. It's why I call the chapters, Laying the Foundation.

Sure, you can go ahead and skip chapters and mimic my process, but will you know the *why* behind my actions? Will you fully understand the terminology I use?

Ideally, this book is a quick read.

To get unstuck, all you need are some basic tools. You

don't have to go from pantser to full-fledged plotter to benefit from plotting.

Whichever path you choose—skipping to the chapters that are interesting to you right now or reading straight through—my hope is that you will be more enthusiastic about your writing than when you first started reading this book.

The priority is to *find your process,* which will reignite your writing fire.

CHAPTER 3 – LAYING THE FOUNDATION, PART II

I had so many unfinished stories.

And So, The Journey Began

Oh, I was great at writing non-fiction and had no problem selling those articles, but fiction? Creating and authoring stories was a whole other art form.

I leaned into the learning of craft and learned about the business of writing, too—the business from the viewpoint of an agent, publisher, or editor. Pre-internet, I joined writing groups, subscribed to magazines, checked out library how-to books, and attended conferences.

What I discovered over time is that those of us who struggled with our stories were missing important plot pillars, deepened characters, emotion, or a combination of all three.

As I journeyed, trying to find my process, I created a plotting workbook, modifying and creating worksheets, directions, and notes, making them work for me.

Today, I can easily spend a month plotting a story, and easily write the first draft in the second month.

Writing is pure joy. I no longer dread writing the first draft. Because of my plotting, I start each story with a 10–to-60 page synopsis outline.

While I had started my fictional writing career as a pantser, over time, I become a plotter.

So, what do those two terms mean?

Pantser, Plotter Definitions

Pantser – Someone who writes without a plot or a plan. If they do have a plan, it's minimal and in their head.

Plotter – Someone who creates a written plan — anywhere from minimal to detailed — before they begin writing their first draft.

Does that mean you have to be one or the other?

No. Not at all.

Today, I'm a mix, a plantser — the term for someone who does both. Even though my fiction and screenplays are highly detailed ahead of time, I still get to pantser the scene in dialogue and movement, where the characters thrive.

Clearing Up the Myths

To determine if my portable storyboard plotting worksheets would work for other writers, I asked a few of my bona fide pantser writer friends if they'd volunteer as beta testers for the worksheets. They were writers who were frustrated because they kept getting stuck along the way or were frustrated by how long it took to write a first draft.

They abhorred the idea of plotting. A few probing questions revealed they'd never tried to plot before. With the promise of all I needed was their feedback, they all were willing to give the worksheets a try.

Once my beta testers used the sheets, pleasantly surprising themselves, they then wanted a one-on-one coaching session that provided more plotting assistance on stories they'd been struggling with.

At the end of our private coaching session, each one sat back, amazed at how easy it was to get unstuck by employing the main plot-point pillars of story but could still enjoy pantsering between these pillars that now provided structure that had been absent. As a result, they were excited about their stories again.

What the Beta Testers Said

"I'm using Diana's Post-it notes plotting sheets to rewrite and revise pantser drafts. Her system defines plot points and calls attention to crucial details for a complete, compelling manuscript. The worksheets are easy-to-use, a real time-saver. They have helped me add depth, find holes, and redefine my stories." – Linda Bradley, author

*****

"I was a skeptical but willing participant because I've been struggling with sagging middles. I found I got a big boost of energy just writing scene ideas on one Post-it after another. I was surprised at how the ideas came so easily.

"By putting the Post-its—I used colored ones—on a big [story] board, I could see plot holes right away. I was shocked to see three of the five major plot points were missing. When pantsering, I would write the book and then have to go back and add content to fix these holes. How much easier it is seeing the holes before I've even begun writing!

"By trying this plotting method on a novella first, I can see how easy it would be to plot out a novel. No more sagging middle! I'm a visual learner and Diana's method has shown me that plotting, which I called outlining, isn't at all like the outlining we used to do in high school classes!" – Diana Lloyd, author

*****

"I couldn't imagine writing my current story as a pantser. When I get ideas and then get stuck, I give up. With Diana's plotting sheets, I could see the possibilities. In the past, I'd run seeing the 12 steps. I didn't understand them or the percentages at key points. Additionally, when putting these 12 steps up on a storyboard with Diana's help, suddenly there were 3 timelines, not just 1 timeline! I can now see the value in plotting a story out, even if not plotting all the minute details." – Linda Fletcher, writer

*****

"I've tried different methods of plotting and various beat sheet methods. Nothing worked well for me. I always felt that something was lacking.

"When I tried Diana's CPE worksheets, I realized I faced a new way of thinking about my story—add emotion to the plot!

"Emotion was the missing component; it drives my characters to make decisions that change the direction of my story. I realized these CPE worksheets gave my story a rudder—a way to drive my plot forward and not wander through the weeds." – L M English, writer

*****

All of these writers had gotten caught in the myths of plotting. Myths wrapped in misinformation, thus creating a wall that they held dear and didn't want to breach.

Myth #1: Plotting is like high school outlining.

Plotting a book looks nothing like the outlining we did in high school. That style of outlining is good for proposals, dissertations, white papers, and other non-fiction projects.

Creating an outline for a book *tells* the story scene by scene in paragraph form. More how-to details are provided in later chapters.

Myth #2: Plotting means there won't be any surprises.

For those who say they like the surprise of pantsering and yet struggle along the way, plotting may be the tool they need to help their writing, even if it's just knowing the ending and the five major plot points, which are prime opportunities to provoke emotion.

Knowing how these pillar placements operate can go a long way toward discovering a character's deep, dark secret.

*****

Plotting holds advantages. Secret advantages. Secret because until you try plotting, a character's secret remains hidden below the surface of the initial story, hidden from viewers, hidden even from the pantsering author in the beginning.

Only by experimenting with plotting—even if at a minimum—can you experience the joy of plotting.

As a heavy plotter, I'm still surprised by my characters when they can make me laugh aloud, tug at my heartstrings, or have me on the edge of my seat in fear as they move through the scene.

You may find that knowing just the backbone of the story improves your pantsering immensely, or you may discover, like me, that you prefer a more detailed plotting process.

Either way, there is no wrong or right way. It's all about what's right *for you!*

DIANA STOUT

CHAPTER 4 – LAYING THE FOUNDATION, PART III

My writing process evolved over time. In this chapter, I share my pantser-to-plotter journey and the experts I encountered along the way.

Journeying Toward the Masters

I'd been writing nonfiction for some time, successfully selling magazine articles, writing a newspaper column, then a magazine column as I dabbled in fiction. I wrote a pile of short stories and sold a few to magazines.

Then, in 1984, I wrote my first book as a pantser. Writing that book took me a year and a half. I submitted what I thought was a polished draft—it was probably my second draft—to Harlequin Books. The book was rejected, as it should have been, with Debra Matteucci, the Senior Editor of American Romance writing:

> *Your manuscript does not fit the requirements for American Romance. It is too melodramatic, based on trite misunderstandings among the characters as well as contrived circumstances.*

While I understood what the editor was saying, I wasn't quite sure how to fix the story.

I noticed she hadn't commented on the setting. I told myself that she must have liked the setting. Yes, I'm being facetious; she probably had no such thought, but telling myself she liked it made me feel better about the rejection.

I used the setting in another book, which would become my third book published.

After that 1986 first-book rejection, I tried to write several more books, still as a pantser. Every time I got stuck in the middle of a story, I was unsure of what to do. I felt like I was muddling my way to the end. My fiction writing, unlike my nonfiction writing, was slow and agonizing.

By 1990, I was living in Tallahassee, then in Cairo, Georgia and was in a writing critique group with two other writers—Jan, a published Avalon romance author and Carole, an unpublished romance writer like myself. We'd meet twice a month, critiquing and editing each other's work. Finally, I could finish the books I'd previously started because I was plotting them out with their brainstorming assistance. They saw plot holes that were invisible to me and helped me develop likeable characters.

In short order, we decided to critique synopses rather than entire books because a synopsis was shorter and easier to read and critique, than it was to read and critique a full novel that had numerous flaws and holes.

We learned to write emotion-filled tight synopses that later became our outlines. By critiquing our synopses, not only were we fixing holes and character issues ahead of time, but we were also writing faster.

More importantly, I was no longer getting stuck. By outlining and writing the synopsis first, I noticed I no longer was dealing with the sagging middle or plot holes.

We'd read each other's entire book only after we believed it was ready for publication. To that end, we became each other's line editor. We were developmental editors with the synopsis critiques and line editors once the books were written.

Back then, agents and publishers wanted queries, accompanied with a partial, which consisted of a synopsis and the first three chapters. Because of our synopsis writing, all three of us were receiving *send me the book* responses to our queries. We were now submitting more polished books that required little editing from the publishers' editors.

Jan continued to publish, and both Carole and I became published.

In the early 1990s, I began winning writing awards,

then sold my first books. At the same time, I started writing screenplays, attended screenwriting film festivals, read as many scripts as I could get my hands on, and paid attention to what Hollywood producers were buying and why.

Based on my published books, I was asked to teach creative writing classes both at a local college and through an online writing community.

*****

By the mid-90s, I started applying screenwriting techniques to my books, surprised at how my writing changed.

I couldn't help but notice how those screenwriting techniques and my discovery of the Hollywood pillars of story structure allowed me to write faster and with a more active first draft.

I would never fully pantser another book again.

Expert Encounters

And then, in the spring of 1997, I had my biggest *aha moments* ever, thanks to Hollywood screenwriter and script consultant, Michael Hauge. I attended his Atlanta weekend workshop that focused on creating characters who were deeply tied to a story's plot. Essentially, he showed us how to develop characters and plot in tandem.

I went home brain dead, but it was during that

weekend when I discovered character is plot and that plot is character.

Character = Plot

Plot = Character

I was already hooked and had been writing taglines based on **Jon Franklin's**, *Writing for Story*, where I had learned how to:

- condense any story into just three words, from which I'd then create
- the tagline/logline sentence, to
- writing a sentence for each main plot point, to
- writing a blurb description, to
- adding a few more sentences to each plot point, turning each point into its own paragraph.

Essentially, I was using a method that a decade later **Randy Ingermanson** would coin as the Snowflake Method in his 2014 book, *How to Write a Novel Using the Snowflake Method*.

The Snowflake Method of plotting is taking a few words or a phrase and adding a sentence or two, growing the idea into more specific details. My example above with the three-word plot and then turning the three words into a couple sentences or a brief paragraph is part of the Snowflake Method.

Just as a snowflake is built from a single crystal, your

story is built from a single idea.

As my plotting journey progressed into more screenwriting, I began reading more screenwriting how-to books and attending screenwriting conferences, thus learning from a new medium of writers, all of whom I consider masters of their fields.

*****

The Masters

Aristotle

Author of *Poetics* – he writes about story as three acts: the beginning, the middle, and the end. He was the first to identify in writing what others were doing organically.

Syd Field

Author of Screenplay (1979) – a screenwriter and professor, who pioneered the screenplay paradigm, which became the Hollywood standard, from which others built upon. His structural foundation took Aristotle's three acts and made the middle as two parts, with all four parts of the three acts of equal measure.

Field employed Pinch Points, which occurred half-way in each of the two Act II sections as a place to remind the audience of the approaching threats as brief scenes from the antagonist's point of view.

Joseph Campbell

Author of *The Power of Myth* (1988) and *The Hero with a Thousand Faces* (1949) – a writer who examined and named the various myths and archetypes, showing how their patterns relate to story. His books inspired Christopher Vogler.

Michael Hauge

Author of *Writing Screenplays That Sell* (1988) – a screenwriter, producer, instructor, and writing coach. I've attended several of his weekend workshops, most recently participating in the beta version of his StorySelling Workshop that is now offered as a full course, and have attended half a dozen or more of his presentations. His newsletters are rich in character building and plot development advice.

Hauge states there are five plot points where the writer can "elicit maximum emotion" from the reader. He named these plot points (with their percentage occurrence in the story) as:

- New Opportunity (10%)
- Change of Plans (25%) – start of Act II, Part 1
- Point of No Return (50%) – start of Act II, Part 2
- Major Setback (75%) – start of Act III
- Climax (90-99%)

IMPORTANT NOTE: These five points of maximum emotion are key to any query or synopsis, especially a short synopsis. Without them, the query or synopsis is doomed to fail, as is any story. In fact, you'll see me repeating this list in other chapter discussions because these five plot points are *key* to every story.

Christopher Vogler
Author of *The Writer's Journey* (1992) – a screenwriter and development executive, Vogler was working for Disney when he set Campbell's hero's journey into 12 story plot points for screenwriters to follow.

This book became my gold standard for plotting.

Vogler's 12 plot points and terminology, with percentage indicators in parentheses that match Hauge's 5 major plot points are:

1. Ordinary World
2. Call to Adventure (10%)
3. Refusal
4. Meeting the Mentor
5. Crossing the Threshold (25%)
6. Tests, Allies, & Enemies
7. Approaching the Innermost Cave (50%)
8. Supreme Ordeal
9. Reward
10. Road Back (75%)
11. Resurrection (90-99%)
12. Return with the Elixir

When using Vogler's screenwriting paradigm and applying it to fiction writing, I was amazed at how much better my writing became. Soon after reading his hot-off-the-press book in 1992 and applying his paradigm to my stories, I began selling my first books to traditional publishers.

Vogler's book is still in high demand and continues to be at the top of the Best Sellers ranking list on Amazon. The 25th anniversary edition, which was a 4th edition, was published in 2020. If I were teaching creative writing in the classroom again, this book would be required reading for the class.

John Truby

Author of *The Anatomy of Story: 22 Steps to Becoming a Master Storyteller* (2007) and *The Anatomy of Genres* (2022) – Screenwriter, story consultant, and instructor of screenwriting classes. I became aware of Truby's 22 steps when I received an early handwritten manuscript copy of what would become his 2007 published book from a producer who was interested in my first screenplays and who was helping me improve my storytelling.

Truby's 22 steps are masterful, his software program of genres incredible.

Over time, however, I found these 22 steps more complex than I wanted to use. I have, though, returned to Truby with his more recent book, *The Anatomy of Genres* and highly recommend it.

Truby is an expert at revealing the *must-have* elements readers want in any given genre. Consequently, his material is extensive.

Blake Snyder

Author of *Save the Cat!* (2005) – A screenwriter and producer, Snyder called his story plot points *beats* and added 3 more. Today, a *beat sheet* is an encapsulation of the plot points.

Snyder's 15 beats, with the 3 additions italicized, are:

1. *Opening Image*
2. *Stating the Theme*
3. Setup
4. Catalyst
5. Debate
6. Break Into 2
7. B Story
8. Fun & Games
9. Midpoint
10. Bad Guys Close In
11. All is Lost
12. Dark Night of the Soul
13. Break into 3
14. Finale
15. *Final Image*

Snyder also introduced The Five-Step Finale:
1. The team plans to make a rescue, meaning they will be infiltrating enemy territory.
2. The plan begins and they move into the heart of the enemy's territory, thus "storming the castle."
3. They reach their target position and discover they're trapped.
4. They have to come up with a new plan.
5. The new plan is put into motion and succeeds.

Jessica Brody continued Snyder's work with her book, *Save the Cat! Writes a Novel* (2018), applying the beats toward fictional books.

Her website has some fantastic how-to articles, and I especially enjoy using her *beat calculator* that dictates on what pages the various plot points should occur — a handy tool when your approximate word count can be converted into beat pages.

> NOTE: While I have referred to Snyder and Brody's steps as beats here in this section, elsewhere in this book, I call these beats *plot points*.

Allen Palmer

Screenwriter and script consultant – When I came across Palmer's 12 Steps of the Hero's Emotional Journey as applied to Vogler's list of 12 plot points, I experienced a huge *aha moment* that, for me, cemented emotion to character, which affected plot.

Palmer's one-word list for the 12 plot points, succinctly summarizes what the main character should be feeling *emotionally*. His list is a masterpiece. Again, notice the key plot point percentages, I put into the list.

1. Ordinary World - *feeling incomplete*
2. Call to Adventure (10%) – *feeling unsettled*
3. Refusal – *feeling resistant*
4. Meeting the Mentor – *feeling encouraged*
5. Crossing the First Threshold (25%) – *feeling committed*
6. Tests, Allies, & Enemies – *feeling disoriented*
7. Approaching the Innermost Cave (50%) –

feeling inauthentic
8. Supreme Ordeal – *feeling confronted*
9. Reward – *feeling reborn*
10. Road Back (75%) – *feeling desperate*
11. Resurrection (90-99%) – *feeling decisive,* showing how they've changed
12. Return with the Elixir – *feeling complete*

*****

As I progressed through my plotting journey, discovering new experts who had renamed Vogler's plot points, I found the different terminology confusing at times.

Even more confusing, for me, were Snyder's percentages, which didn't line up exactly to Hauge's five main plot points and their percentages.

Because I needed a visual of these various terms to end my confusion, I created a Comparison of Experts chart of Vogler, Hauge, and Snyder's plot points, and Palmer's feelings for Vogler's 12 plot points.

I've shifted Snyder's plot points slightly, so that the events matched up percentagewise with Vogler's and Hauge's.

While Syd Field's two Pinch Points—at 37% and 62%—aren't in this grid, they are listed in Chapter 9, where the descriptions of each plot point are discussed thoroughly.

CPE

Syd Field & % location	Chris Vogler	Blake Snyder	Michael Hauge	Allen Palmer (Feelings)
Act I		Opening Image		
	Ordinary World	Setup		Incomplete
3%		Theme Stated	Throwaway line	
10%	Call to Adventure	Catalyst	New Opportunity	Unsettled
	Refusal of the Call	Debate		Resistant
	Meeting the Mentor	Break Into 2		Encouraged
Act II Part I 25%	Crossing the First Threshold	B Story	Change of Plans	Committed
	Tests, Allies, Enemies	Fun & Games		Disoriented
Act II Part 2 50%	Approach to the Innermost Cave	Midpoint	Point of No Return	Inauthentic
	Supreme Ordeal	Guys Close In		Confronted
	Seizing the Reward	Break Into 3		Reborn
Act III 75%	The Road Back	All is Lost Dark Night of the Soul	Major Setback	Desperate
90-99%	Resurrection	Finale 5-Part Finale	Climax	Decisive
	Return home w/Elixir	Final Image		Complete

Figure 1: Comparison of Experts Chart

Because these primary plot points are known by multiple names as shown in Figure 1's Comparison of Experts chart, for my purposes and for my plotting sheets that you'll see later, I changed the 5-part finale plan to 4-parts and chose a name for each plot point that made the most sense to me. They are:

CPE Plot Points

Act I
- Ordinary World
- Throwaway Line (3%)
- New Opportunity (10%)
- Discussion & Decision
- Meeting the Mentor

Act II
- Change of Plans (25%)
- Tests, Allies, & Enemies
- Pinch Point (37%)
- Midpoint Self-Reflection (50%)
- First Battle
- Pinch Point (62%)
- Celebration (False Win)

Act III
- Major Setback Where All is Lost (75%)
- Climax (90-99%) which includes:
    - Part 1: Finale Plan
    - Part 2: Finale Charge
    - Part 3: Finale Trapped
    - Part 4: Finale Battle
- Claiming the Prize

CHAPTER 5 – LAYING THE FOUNDATION, PART IV

Other Important Elements

What follows in this chapter are key storytelling elements that are important to the story but aren't significant to any one particular listed plot point. They are elements that can be important to the developing plot or character arc.

Backstory

Before the hero or heroine's story journey begins, there is backstory.

As a new writer who was pantsering, I started at the beginning as everyone does, which was getting to know the character, talking about how she got to where we—she and I—were starting the story.

When a mentor told me that I needed to cut the first three chapters of that first book—the equivalent of 60 pages and 15,000 words—I was horrified. She told me it was all backstory.

Sadly, she was right.

Starting a book with backstory is the worst and most

boring way to begin.

Many of us are guilty of writing backstory when starting a new project. It's what we do. We're wanting to know the situation *and* the characters, but I've learned that while backstory information is important to my plotting, it's not important for the readers to know yet. They'll learn about it later in the story.

Not so with literary writing. Often, these books start with backstory, and it works. Backstory doesn't always work well in commercial fiction, though.

The goal is to start with immediate action or meaningful dialogue, working the problem into the Ordinary World.

So, how does one avoid starting a story with backstory?

Write the backstory but don't put it into the book. Not right away. Consider it research for you for now. It won't be wasted material; you'll be using it later.

Ghost Event / Ghost Person
Discovery / Backstory

All people, characters too, are haunted, *wounded* by something that occurred in the past. It could have been an event gone bad, something traumatic or so terrifying that the main character still has nightmares about it. Over time, the ghost event or ghost person is diminished for everyone but the main character for whom it became buried or lost in the progress of time. Hence, the term *ghost* is appropriate.

Ideally, backstory ghost information is spread throughout the book like cookie crumbs, eventually leading us to the ghost event or ghost person reveal, where the backstory began.

A ghost person could be an ex-lover, someone who left them standing at the altar. The ghost person could have been a playground bully or a parent who betrayed them. The ghost event could have been a traumatic event of abuse, losing a job, being evicted, having served in a war, and pretending everything's fine when it isn't, and so forth.

The importance of knowing your main character's ghost before you draft the story is knowing how the ghost lurks in the shadows and affects the character's decision making and the truths by which they live. The character has never talked about this wound before and has carried it through time. Consequently, this story has the character butting up against this wound multiple times. It's a secret they never wanted revealed.

From the beginning and from an emotional standpoint, we see that the character's reactions are slightly off, without knowing why. Something doesn't make sense, and we become curious about the why. Eventually, as the ghost is revealed, we gain understanding and learn what the character was hiding.

From the first page of your story, the character must be making decisions, and their wound will be affecting their decisions even though we, the readers, aren't aware of the wound yet.

The character cannot be acted upon. Take, for example, where a character has just been told they have to work Christmas Eve despite any family plans they've made.

Is the character is being acted upon? While it may feel that way, the character has been given a choice to make:

- To work, canceling their plans and keeping their job.
- To not work, knowing they risk being fired.

Lots of Christmas romance movies start this way, but it's a decision the main character is making. Thus, in canceling their plans, they usually travel back home or to some other destination where they meet up with their ghost.

Not all movies and books are that obvious with the character's ghost. An extreme opposite is the *Star Wars* series, where Luke isn't even aware that the villain he fights is a ghost from his past. The audience is just as surprised as Luke with the revelation.

Good Will Hunting is an excellent example of a character having a ghost event. Will's actions and decisions evolved from a repeated childhood situation that Will has stuffed so far down in his psyche that it takes a psychology professor and counselor to unearth and bring to light this ghost event that Will fights to keep hidden.

Your goal as a writer is to have the reader purchase the book or have the agent, editor, or publisher want to request and read the entire manuscript after reading just a few pages. That goal is rarely achieved when a story starts with an information dump.

Additionally, the worst ways to begin a story is to have a character:

- Waking up
- Getting out of the shower
- Driving somewhere
- Looking in the mirror and reflecting
- Describing the day, the room, or the weather

Consider starting your story with action or dialogue with a second person, where the main character is confronted with a minor problem, which leads us organically into the larger problem.

Ghost Triggers

Plot Triggers are designed to bring up emotions tied to the character's wound. It's their emotions to these triggers that control their decisions in the first part of the story.

As the story progresses, we see their inner battle as they start confronting that ghost, as their actions are changing, and as they move through their character arc, becoming the person they've desired.

Ideally, you want a trigger that can be engaged three times.

Key Question

Before you begin drafting your story, consider the overall question being asked of the story, a question which needs to be answered by the story's end.

Thus, the Key Question is tied to every scene either through character or by plot events.

Examples:

> *Jaws*: Can Brody save his community from a killer shark?
>
> *Saving Private Ryan*: Can Captain Miller and his team find Private Ryan and get him home safely?
>
> *Day After Tomorrow*: Can Jack Hall be there for his son?

In the beginning of *Day After Tomorrow*, we see how Jack Hall has repeatedly not been there for his son:

always late or never attending important moments. And then, in this story, he's up against huge odds of needing to rescue his son. Can he do it?

Magic of Three (3)

As you think about your story, consider an object or action that can be used at least three times. Did you notice how I earlier suggested using a ghost trigger three times?

Repeatedly, the magic of three is used in fairy tales and nursery rhymes: Three Little Pigs, Sleeping Beauty's three fairy godmothers, Goldilocks and the Three Bears, genies and godmothers granting three wishes, Ebenezer's visits from three ghosts...

The Magic of Three ties a story together easily with a seamless continuity. It's a simple way of adding meaningful scenes or layering into an existing scene, creating more depth.

This powerful magic-of-three tool can be used as a motif, as symbolism, as a trait, or be tied to setting or a situation, as well.

Examples:

> *Hunger Games* – Over time, Katniss becomes as powerful as her greatest enemies, and she does it through the bow and arrow as she...
>
> 1. hunts for illegal game to feed her family.

2. spears the apple in the roasted pig's mouth sitting on the Gamemakers' table to get their attention.
   3. destroys her opponents' store of supplies.

In the sequels, the bow and arrow are used again multiple times and in powerful plot-changing ways.

Titanic – The Heart of the Ocean necklace is shown more than three times in the past story and three times in the present story:

Past:
   1. When Rose is gifted the necklace by her fiancé, Cal.
   2. When she poses nude with the necklace.
   3. When the necklace is slipped into Jack's pocket without his knowledge.
   4. When Rose discovers the necklace in the coat pocket after she's been rescued from the *Titanic*.

Present:
   1. As the recovery crew opens a safe and sees a sketching of a nude woman wearing the necklace.
   2. When showing elderly Rose her nude portrait.
   3. When Rose tosses the necklace overboard.

Grendel's Mother – In my fantasy that shows how a

character from *Beowulf* who had no voice was actually human and not a monster as many films have depicted her, the dandelion became a symbol.

1. She blows on a dandelion with seeds and is chastised by her mother who tells the myth that now someone will die.
2. She plucks a dandelion from the ground just before she's grabbed from behind.
3. She makes dandelion tea.
4. A young Grendel gives her a bouquet of dandelions, some new, some barely open, others gone to seed. He blows them into her face.
5. When Beowulf steps out of the water to fight her, a dandelion is stuck in his medieval chain mail shirt.
6. In the end, she realizes she *is* the dandelion, never forgotten, always seen in spring as life blossoms again. Those who vanquished her can never forget or get rid of her.

Out of Africa – This beautiful love story has several motifs: the coffee plants, the water, and Karen's hair, and each one is used at least three times.

For example, her hair:

1. Karen arrives in Africa, perfectly coiffed, with not a hair out of place.
2. As the story progresses, her hair becomes as wild as Africa.

3. And then, when she goes on safari with Denys, he's washing her hair because it has become so entangled, she can't even get a comb through it—representing much of her life in Africa.

Can you see how an object not only injects itself into a story, but into a character's perspective, their truth, and even the theme?

Why Today?

One of the most important questions you need to ask and answer both from a character and plot stance is *Why today?*

Your Chapter 1 should answer within a few pages *why today*, as the story begins with a small conflict that grows and escalates as the story continues.

Prologue

Some stories require a short prologue to reveal an event tied to backstory that will answer Chapter 1's *why today?*

In my book, *Love's New Beginning*, the prologue shows the main character being robbed, her arm broken, and receiving a concussion from hitting her head on the cement. What we don't see between the prologue and Chapter 1 is her hospitalization, her boyfriend/agent emptying her bank accounts and deserting her, and her grandfather's death and funeral.

Chapter 1 starts with her at the lawyer's office, learning the contents of her grandfather's will and dealing with its requirements. It's the contents of this will *and* the results of the robbery that tell *why today* and starts the motion of what is about to happen, which has her butting up against her wound repeatedly throughout the story.

Not all stories, however, need a prologue.

Prologues are common place in mysteries and psychological thrillers where the audience needs to see the earlier crime taking place, setting up the main character's entrance into the crime that will concern or affect the main character's wound.

The prologue event can dovetail into the main character's New Opportunity, their New Beginning, or with the Antagonist.

A prologue is never long. It's a brief scene that shows and sets up the danger that is lurking out there for the main character, or it reveals an event from the past that affects today's seemingly small conflict in the Ordinary World.

KEY: The prologue is designed to reveal emotional danger, physical danger, psychological danger, or all three together.

*****

A reminder as we move into each pillar of structural

storytelling…

Plot is how we become interested in reading the book or seeing the movie. The storyline intrigues us.

Character is how we become engaged in a story. The protagonist is either like us or is someone we'd like to become. We can relate to their situation or are fascinated by it, wanting it to happen to us or hoping it never will.

Emotion is the magic ingredient that connects us to both character and plot. If the book or movie can make us gasp, cry, laugh, sigh, or have us sitting on the edge of our seats, it's a story we'll tell others about. We're passionate about sharing our experiences.

CHAPTER 6 – CHARACTER

Every scene of any story needs to do at least one of two things: show character, and/or move plot forward.

Generally, the main character serves the story in one of two ways:

- as an ordinary character in an extraordinary world or situation.
- as an extraordinary character in an ordinary world.

Ordinary / Extraordinary

Examples of ordinary characters in an extraordinary world or situation:

- *The Santa Claus,* where a father accidentally evaporates Santa, who leaves his suit behind with a note that forces the father to wear the suit, thus becoming Santa. Dad, an ordinary citizen, is forced into an extraordinary world filled with magic, becoming extraordinary himself.

- *Gone with the Wind,* where Scarlett O'Hara and Rhett Butler, who start out as a tad extraordinary from the other characters simply because they don't follow traditional rules, are caught in the extraordinary backdrop of the Civil War.

- *The Hunger Games*, where Katniss Everdeen is placed into an impossible extraordinary competition.

- *All the President's Men*, where two ordinary reporters doggedly follow evidence that leads to an extraordinary investigation culminating in a U.S. President having to resign before he becomes impeached.

- *The Hunt for Red October*, where an ordinary Russian submarine captain defects to America with the submarine and an unsuspecting crew, thus creating an extraordinary situation and who is surprised to discover that the Americans want to aid him in that defection.

Extraordinary characters can include those holding high offices such as a President, royalty, or being placed into an extraordinary situation, such as facing off against a higher power, in an otherwise ordinary world. Or, they can be extraordinary because they are endowed with extraordinary skills or powers. Examples of extraordinary characters are:

- *E.T.*, an alien left behind and who befriends a young boy who helps him get back home. Elliot, the young boy, is the ordinary character dealing with an extraordinary character.

- Edward in *Twilight*, a vampire who falls in love with an ordinary girl who befriends his vampire family, eventually marrying him, thus entering Edward's extraordinary world.

- Gerry Lane (Brad Pitt) in *World War Z*, as a former expert United Nations Investigator (deemed as one of the best, which makes him extraordinary), and who needs to secure his family's safe passage while he troubleshoots the zombie pandemic and while trying to find a cure against this deadly disease, which will aid both his family and the world.

- President James Marshall (Harrison Ford) in *Air Force One* as an extraordinary person who then becomes trapped in an extraordinary terrorist-filled situation where he attempts to save his family and the planeload of people who work with him.

- In *The American President*, President Andrew Shepherd (Michael Douglas) as an extraordinary character, working in an ordinary Washington D.C. world, tries to journey through the political landscape and a new love relationship, realizing he needs to be even more extraordinary by doing the right thing regardless of the costs.

The scope of these last three examples sets main characters and situations in the extraordinary scale simply by virtue of their careers and events they're dealing with. And yet, at the same time, these are ordinary people in extraordinary jobs—meaning not everyone has the ability or wants to perform these jobs. It's the extraordinary elements that make these stories so attractive to audiences.

BMOC

Peter Russell, a script doctor, teacher, and story analyst, coined story as the BMOC—beginning, middle, obstacle, and climax. He states that movie goers don't care about the plot nearly as much as they care about the character.

Consequently, we begin to care about the main character in their Ordinary World, at the beginning of the story.

We are emotionally invested in their journey by the middle of the story and with every obstacle they face.

We are on the edge of our seats as the character fights to overcome the climax, providing us with a satisfying resolution.

Consider the BMOCs of memorable characters such as:

- Rhett Butler and Scarlett O'Hara
- Woody & Buzz Lightyear
- Elizabeth Bennett and Mr. Darcy
- Sherlock Holmes
- Katniss Everdeen

- Harry Potter
- Atticus Finch & Scout
- Cinderella
- Heathcliff and Cathy
- E.T.
- Forrest Gump
- Freddy Krueger
- Frankenstein
- Indiana Jones
- Hannibal Lecter
- Captain Jack Sparrow
- Scrooge & Tiny Tim
- Luke Skywalker, Hans Solo, & Darth Vader
- Dorothy, Scarecrow, Cowardly Lion, & the Tin Man

These are just a few of the many memorable characters in literary and movie history. No doubt, you have your own favorites. These characters are memorable for us because they stirred our emotions at the beginning, deepened those emotions by the middle, and had us solidly invested by the climax.

Character Arcs

Generally, the ordinary main character will grow by finally confronting their ghost; that growth is known as a character arc.

Those extraordinary characters who can be classified as superheroes rarely have an arc; instead, it's the ordinary characters they engage with who will experience an arc.

Laurie Schnebly Campbell, author, writing coach, and instructor, states in her October 30, 2023, *Writers in the Storm* blog, "Mastering Character Evolution: A Power Ladder of Choice," that the main character will "have to cover each step of their journey…

> from Stasis
> to Change
> through Misdirection
> to Recovery
> through Reversion
> to Realization
> then Triumph."

Sometimes that arc is nothing more than overcoming a fear based on a prior event, as occurs for Jack Ryan in *The Hunt for Red October* as he overcomes multiple flying fears, all because of horrendous injuries and a lengthy recovery, the result of a helicopter accident.

In *World War Z*, Gerry Lane's struggle is in wanting to protect his family first; but to protect them, he needs to help the world, which means he's depending on others to protect his family in his place. His character arc was more about overcoming the extraordinary challenges and struggles of finding a possible cure and helping others deal with their fears along the way.

The best stories embrace this extraordinary element

that pushes characters into scary roles and activities, forcing them to survive, whether they begin as ordinary or extraordinary characters.

Also, most of these stories are based on survival in one form or another, which becomes its own plot device.

Other Primary Characters

As I've mentioned earlier, in 1997, while attending **Michael Hauge**'s weekend workshop in Alanta, I had a huge *aha moment*. The workshop was based on his 1988 book, *Writing Screenplays that Sell,* where he presented a chart of the main character and three supporting primary characters.

The four characters (with other terminology) are:
- The Hero (Protagonist)
- The Nemesis (Antagonist)
- The Reflection / Buddy (Mentor)
- The Romance (Love Interest / Fake Antagonist)

With this chart drawn on the board, he drew arrows as I've replicated here to show how these three core characters are tied to the hero's Inner Conflict—the inner emotional wound—and how each of the other three's motivational goals feed into the main character's wound, finally forcing the hero to deal with that wound.

	Outer Motivation	Outer Conflict	Inner Motivation	Inner Conflict
Hero				
Nemesis				
Reflection/ Buddy				
Romance				

Figure 2: Hauge 1988 motivation & character chart

This was the piece of storytelling that I'd been missing when creating characters! Nearly 30 years later, I can still feel that *aha moment* as if it had occurred yesterday; it was that profound.

I could see why my earlier characters had been shallow and moved around like paper dolls.

The movie analysis Hauge used, along with his chart of these four primary characters with their goals, motivations, and conflicts allowed me to see how characters interact with each other *because* of their connection to the protagonist's wound.

To unpack this diagram a little...

The Outer Motivation represents the tangible goal.

The Outer Conflict is the visible struggle in trying to achieve that visible/tangible goal. The Outer Conflict will always be with another person, institution, rule, law, standard, or an element in nature. Something the character can't control.

The Inner Motivation represents *why* the goal is *wanted.*

The Inner Conflict represents what the character *needs, and why it's needed*. The Inner Conflict *is* all about the character's wound.

It's okay if you don't quite understand this chart right away. Better understanding will come in this continued analysis of the characters here and when I show how I use the chart in Chapter 11.

For now, let's look at each of these four important story characters more closely.

The Hero (Protagonist)

Hauge contends that everything a protagonist thinks, says, and does goes back to just one thing—their wound and how the wound more often than not occurred in the character's youth. That event is backstory and will be leaked as the story progresses.

Because of that wound, the character formed a belief, actually a lie they live by, and then they butt up against the lie/wound several times throughout the story. The wound is rarely an in-your-face kind of wound, but one that is more subtle, not easily detected.

While a main character's external goal will become known immediately in the Ordinary World, their internal goal (Inner Motivation), the unspoken reason why the character is pursuing that goal won't be revealed right away. Generally, the reveal occurs at the Midpoint plot point, which is also called a Mirror Moment.

An example of such a character is Christian Grey, who lives a lie in *Fifty Shades of Grey*. He believes he's no good in a relationship, so he lives a secret life outside of and unlike his extraordinary business success. It takes a strong heroine to show him he is worthy of a relationship.

Sam Wheat (Patrick Swayze) in *Ghost* is another example. He believes he doesn't deserve good things let alone love. When his girlfriend, Mollie, asks if he's worried about their moving in together, he responds, "Whenever something good in my life happens to me, I'm just afraid I'm going to lose it" (p. 16)[1]. That's the first time she says, "I love you," and he replies, "Ditto." He can't say the words because he doesn't fully believe yet. The theme of the story is how one can show love without saying the words. Throughout the movie, he's showing his love in trying to protect her. In the end, he overcomes his wound when he says for the first time, *I love you*.

The protagonist's Internal Conflict—their wound— won't be fully revealed until much later in the story,

---

[1] Ghost (1990) screenplay, retrieved from https://assets.scriptslug.com/live/pdf/scripts/ghost-1990.pdf.

but until that final reveal, bits and pieces of the ghost event or ghost person will be dropped along the story path just like Hansel and Gretel's bread crumbs.

The protagonist's wound is the deep well from which the story draws upon.

*****

The Nemesis (Antagonist / True Villian)

Generally, this character is embodied by the protagonist's Inner Conflict even though the antagonist's Outer Motivation (goal) appears to conflict only with the protagonist's Outer Motivation (goal).

If the nemesis isn't responsible for the hero's wound, then the nemesis' Outer Motivation (outer goal) embodies the hero's wound in some way.

There aren't many stories where the antagonist is the main character, but one such antagonist is the Joker, a deeply wounded supervillain, who was driven insane, and who turns to crime wanting to hurt others, thus creating chaos in Gotham City. Two such versions of this character are portrayed in:

- The 2008, *The Dark Knight,* starring Heath Ledger, who won an Oscar for his role posthumously.
- The 2019, *Joker,* starring Joaquin Phoenix.

Typically, the antagonist is an enemy of the protagonist. Both have equal power to fight each other, but in the beginning, it will appear as if the villain has more power. It's only as the protagonist arcs into their essence, the truth of their inner core, that they can see the possibility of overcoming their internal wound and defeating the villain.

*****

The Reflection / Buddy (Mentor)

The buddy character asks the main character, *You know what your problem is?*

This buddy character doesn't wait for an answer but will answer the rhetorical question immediately after asking it. Generally, the answer is integral to the *theme* of the story and relates to the *key question* the story is answering.

Also, the answer feeds into the story's conflict, the character's external goal, and is attached to several plot points.

This buddy character *knows* of the main character's wound, which is why they can ask: *Do you know what your problem is?* and be able to state the truth of what the main character needs. This conversation can contain the throwaway line within the first 3% of the story. It'll sound like ordinary dialogue, but it's tied to the protagonist's past behavior. Ideally, this throwaway dialogue line tells the audience what this story is going to be about.

Of course, the protagonist laughs it off or ignores the answer, because the lie they believe is far removed from this truth they're hearing.

This important buddy character is a best friend, or someone the protagonist respects, someone with authority, such as a teacher, neighbor, or a wise person in the community.

This buddy character gives advice—often unasked—and will readily tell the character when they're screwing up later. They'll tell their friend what they don't want to hear—the truth.

This buddy character is there to help the protagonist achieve their goal and can easily forgive any stubborn rudeness because the buddy character cares deeply about the protagonist. We're *shown* the depth of their relationship as they journey through the story.

Above all, this buddy character never lies; they always tell the main character the truth, often against their will.

An example:

In *The American President,* President Andrew Shepherd argues with Chief of Staff and best friend, A.J. MacInerney, about wanting to keep his new relationship private, and then A.J. criticizes Andrew, where Andrew swears and gets angry. Starting to walk out, he stops and asks, *If Mary* (his wife at the time he first ran for President) *hadn't died, would we have won three years ago?*

A.J.: *Would we have won?*

Shepherd: *If we had to go through a character debate three years ago, would we have won?*

A.J.: *I don't know. But I would have liked that campaign if my friend Andy Shepherd had shown up. I would have liked that campaign very much.*[2]

An important exchange because it shows they've had discussions like this before, where one becomes angry and one doesn't; where Shepherd respects A.J. because despite his anger, Shepherd stops and asks the question, wanting to know the truth; and where A.J. is telling Shepherd through subtext that the man standing in front of him at this moment isn't the friend that A.J. respects and loves.

*****

Romance (Love Interest, (Fake) Antagonist)

The romance character embodies a push/pull relationship with the main character. One popular network's holiday movies are based on this premise.

---

[2] "The American President, 1995. *Quotes*. Website: https://www.quotes.net/mquote/1078253. January 3, 2024.

Most traditional romances, books and movies both, embody this premise, too.

This romance character, which I've dubbed as a Love Interest and as a Fake Antagonist, often appears in opposition to the main character but then becomes a love interest. Consequently, this character can be viewed as both.

This character can alternate siding with the main character or standing against them as they work through their conflicting goals.

Other examples of the Romance / Love Interest / (Fake Antagonist) character can be seen in:

- *Romancing the Stone* – Jack T. Colton (Michael Douglas)
- *Pride and Prejudice* – Mr. Darcy
- *A Walk to Remember* – Landon Carter (Shane West)
- *You've Got Mail* – Joe Fox, (Tom Hanks)
- *The Proposal* – Andrew Paxton (Ryan Renolds)

DIANA STOUT

CHAPTER 7 – PLOT

I'd always understood that Story A was about the main character and that Story B was about antagonist and the conflict they brought into Story A. But then, I found a different take on Story A and Story B that made more sense.

Mitchell German

Author of *Your Storytelling Potential: The Underground Guide to Finally Writing a Great Screenplay or Novel* (2023) and the creator of Plot Control, a software program for screenwriting and movie development contends both Story A and Story B are situations.

Situation A centers on what the character wants.

Situation B focuses on what the character needs.

Both situations drive the story with the protagonist sandwiched in between the two situations, which are at odds with each other, as I've depicted in this simple Venn diagram. German states that the character lives in that small overlapping (darker) section and is caught—trapped actually—between the two situations.

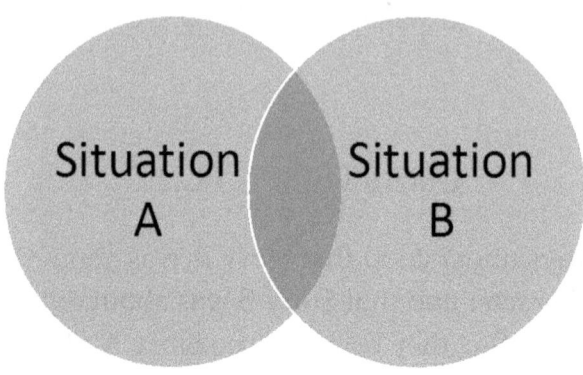

Figure 3: Story A & B

In trying to manage these situations, the protagonist finds themselves traveling toward a collision of their external *want* with their internal *need*, thus they become their own worst enemy. They screw up their job, their family, their predictable life, the people around them while trying to make everyone happy, yet feeling miserable in the process.

Story A is revealed right away as we're introduced to the main character and their goal in their Ordinary World.

If provided a glimpse of Story B in the first act, it resembles the tip of an iceberg that appears above the waterline. There's a lot of ice hidden below the surface, and it's that hidden mass that threatens to swamp and wreak havoc with the character's life throughout the rest of the story. That hidden ice represents their need—their wound.

Examples:

Titanic: Story A is Rose feeling as if she's traveling to America on a slave ship, as she'll be enslaved to Cal who isn't always a nice guy. Story B is her desire to be her own woman, to control her destiny, as encouraged by Jack. Thus, Cal is Story A, Jack is Story B.

Liar, Liar: Story A is lawyer Fletcher Reede always breaking his promise to spend time with his son because of his career. Story B is promising his son that he won't lie to him anymore.

You've Got Mail: Story A is Joe Fox uncaring of businesses that close because of his opening a new branch of his store nearby. Story B is Joe Fox falling for one of those business owners and wanting to help her, but without her knowing he's helping because she can't stand him.

Why We Buy Books and Movie Tickets

Story is why we buy the books and movie tickets. We're enthralled with the high concept story of:

- Terrorists taking control, seizing a tower, a plane, or some other public arena.
- A girl discovering she's a princess and in line to be the next queen.
- An alien having been left behind.
- A teenager in a new school attracted to a vampire.

- A teenager fighting for her life in a contest.
- A father dressing up, pretending to be a maid just so he can see his children that a judge has forbidden him to see but just a couple of weeks each year.
- A young woman discovering she's been dating a prince.

Story drags these characters out of their Ordinary World, moving them into a new outer world that conflicts with their Story B issues, all of which creates the emotion.

CHAPTER 8 – EMOTION

While Story A gets us into the theater seat or onto the book page, it's Story B that turns these stories into favorites because of how the characters and plot combined have engaged our emotions as the protagonist struggles to achieve their goal, while overcoming their past wound.

Emotion as Story's Beating Heart

Emotion is the heart of every story.

Without it, characters will be flat. Dialogue will sound forced or stilted. Events will appear circumstantial or contrived.

The backstory is what sets up the character's emotion. Their wound. It's a deep, dark secret that if revealed will destroy or shame them.

But, it's the heart that keeps that wound alive, keeping the character in constant hidden pain.

While everyone talks about building plot and characters predominately, building emotion doesn't get discussed with the same intensity.

Emotion is the star that stands out among the three

pillars of story, because without it, there isn't a story worth telling.

Great stories are emotion filled.

While the next chapter discusses the plot points in detail, we have to remember Hauge's proclamation of the five major plot points, where the story spins because of the character making choices while trying to ignore the wound at first, and then making choices in an attempt to resolve that wound.

Every plot point event is an opportunity to squeeze character emotion and deepen reader and viewer interest.

An Exercise Worth Trying

Once I became aware of those five big plot points, I started watching movies with a stopwatch in the theater or on DVD. (We didn't have streaming then.)

I'd start the stopwatch as the movie began and note the time on the stopwatch as each of these five major plot points occurred.

> New Opportunity at 10%
> Change of Plans at 25%
> Midpoint Self-Reflection at 50%
> Major Setback Where All is Lost at 75%
> Climax at 90-99%

Once I knew how long the movie was, I could easily

do the math to see if those five plot point events occurred at their designated percentages.

It was a rare movie that didn't come close to these percentages.

The same percentages occur in books, as well.

Not sure? Check it out. I was amazed to discover this writing secret of timing, where all stories follow this plotting structure.

CPE

Chapter 9 – The Plot Points

This chapter is an in-depth discussion of the plot points: what they do, where they occur, who is featured in them, and how to produce more character emotion.

Here is the list of plot point terms I use when plotting, which are on my plotting worksheets in Chapter 10:

CPE Plot Points

Act I
    Ordinary World
    Throwaway Line (3%)
    New Opportunity
    Discussion & Decision
    Meeting the Mentor

Act II
    Change of Plans (25%)
    Tests, Allies, & Enemies
    Pinch Point (37%)
    Midpoint Self-Reflection (50%)
    First Battle
    Pinch Point (62%)
    Celebration (False Win)

Act III
    Major Setback Where All is Lost (75%)

Climax (90-99%) which includes:
    Part 1: Finale Plan
    Part 2: Finale Charge
    Part 3: Finale Trapped
    Part 4: Finale Battle
Claiming the Prize

In this chapter, the headings for these plot point explanations will use the *CPE* name on the first line.

Any lines following are other known plot point names, with additional titles when helpful.

The last line represents that plot point's feeling from Palmer's list.

Your story's genre will depend on how each of these plot points will operate. For example, a romance could have two Ordinary Worlds: one for hero and one for the heroine. The same could occur for a story that has a protagonist and an antagonist where it's important to see the antagonist's world.

Act I

Ordinary World
Setup / Current Life
Feeling Incomplete

The Ordinary World provides a glimpse of the main character's current existence as it occurs at the start of the story. What their life looks like. How they feel, how they interact with others, and any other significant details that help us become sympathetic to this protagonist from the beginning. We need to like this character right away, otherwise, we won't invest our emotions into their journey. So, we need to see them perform an act that reflects kindness or caring.

From this current life, we see that the protagonist is unhappy or dissatisfied with their life. They *feel incomplete*. Something is lacking or they're wanting something wonderful to happen in the future, which they believe will be of their choosing. Otherwise, they feel they'll be stuck in this life forever, something they don't want.

It's in the Ordinary World that we see any special skills the protagonist has. Skills that appear relatively ordinary because of a hobby or interest but will have value when combating the villain later.

Examples of hobbies and skills:
- Sharpshooting
- Stunt driver
- Seamstress
- Magician able to make things disappear
- High-wire acrobat

Examples of having knowledge of:
- Survival skills
- Poisons
- History

- Befriending wild animals

Whatever skill or knowledge they have will be used later, but for that to happen, that skill or knowledge needs to be seen in action within the Ordinary World first, even if we see only a tiny bit. It's best if the skill or knowledge isn't emphasized but appears as something normal or usual.

Keep in mind that the Ordinary World is just as much about place as is the character's current feeling. Yes, they will be leaving the Ordinary World location and could very well be returning to that same location at the end of their journey, but their original Ordinary World *feeling* will be gone because they return as a new person, someone who has grown and moved beyond feeling stuck.

Additionally, not all stories have the protagonist leaving the location of the Ordinary World, but their feelings and attitude about their Ordinary World as they currently live will be left behind.

This is the first time we see a glimpse of the protagonist's fear, but we have no idea where that fear comes from. Not yet.

We don't want an information dump to occur in this Ordinary World setup. We only need to know *how* and *why* the protagonist is feeling incomplete, at this stage. Examples:

- A young woman is tired of always being a bridesmaid and never a bride.
- A teenage boy realizes this is his last year to make the team.
- A single parent hates their job but doesn't believe they can risk quitting.

The Ordinary World begins on the day that is going to be different from every other day, because this is the day they are offered a New Opportunity or serves as a Catalyst, propelling the character to make choices they'd otherwise never make.

Throwaway Line
Theme Stated

Within the Ordinary World, we hear the throwaway line spoken by the Buddy / Reflection character, Mentor, or someone of Authority. Generally, the line is stated early in the story, around the 3% mark.

Michael Hauge was the first to bring my attention to this important line, which is theme-related and stated in dialogue by the buddy character answering their own question of *Do you know what your problem is?* And then, the buddy tells the protagonist what they don't want to hear but has in the past, with the protagonist shrugging it off.

This all-important throwaway line will be masked in ordinary conversation, so we often miss it unless we're looking for it.

Examples:

- *Pride & Prejudice* (2008): While at a community dance, Lizzy Bennett tells her older sister, Jane, that all men are "humorless poppycocks." Jane replies, "One of these days someone will catch your eye and then you'll have to watch your tongue." Enter Mr. Bingley and Mr. Darcy, who gets caught looking Lizzy's way. Lizzy laughs and from Darcy and Lizzy's first conversation, she's determined to speak her mind, and throughout the movie, she's taken to task by her best friend Charlotte Lucas, her mother, her aunt and repeatedly with Mr. Darcy.
- *Dead Poet's Society* – Fellow students ask Neil, "Why doesn't [your father] let you do what you want? Tell him off." Neil responds, "Like you guys tell your parents off." Then later, Professor Keating reinforces in class, "Strive to find your voice. The longer you wait to begin, the less likely you are to find it."
- *World War Z* – On TV, a reporter announces "…declared martial law…" and Dad (Brad Pitt) answers his youngest child's question of "What's martial law?" explaining martial law is like "house rules but for everybody." Ultimately, the theme of survival is about zombies who appear not to follow the rules, yet they do, as Dad figures out in the end. Notice, though, how often Dad breaks the rules in his determination to find a way for humanity to survive this zombie virus.

New Opportunity (10%)
Call to Adventure / Catalyst
Feeling Unsettled

While a New Opportunity at first feels exciting and desired, after thinking about it for a bit, that excitement dissipates; they're *feeling unsettled*.

A New Opportunity means facing an unknown, and the protagonist become suspicious, subtly fearful about what they don't know.

Discussion & Decision
Refusal of the Call / Debate
Feeling Resistant

Here is where the protagonist talks out their confusion with everyone except their mentor: what should they do?

There's the tug of staying true to their current responsibilities, even if it's a life not of their desire or passion. They're still *feeling resistant* to making a change.

The emotional struggle needs to be shown.

On the flip side, if the New Opportunity is accepted at this point, it's because they've either lost everything or fear they're about to lose it all.

Meeting the Mentor
Break into 2
Feeling Encouraged

In having rejected the New Opportunity, they're willing to talk it out with their buddy, a mentor, or someone of authority that they respect.

This all-important person won't lie and tells the protagonist the stark truth.

Regardless if the protagonist had turned down the New Opportunity or accepted it, after meeting with their mentor, they're *feeling encouraged* about their decision. Until...

Something occurs that forces them to now accept the New Opportunity if they had previously turned it down.

Act II – Part I

Change of Plans (25%)
Crossing the First Threshold / B Story
Feeling Committed

This plot point is ripe for emotion through action or dialogue and is pivotal because it's where the character is *feeling committed* to the decision, having fully accepted the New Opportunity.

- In *World War Z*, this is where Dad learns if he

doesn't accept the New Opportunity, his family won't be safe, so he accepts. Keeping his family safe is his first priority.

- In *Star Wars*, this is where Luke feels confused after meeting with Obi-Wan and returns home to find his family and home destroyed. This spot is where Luke accepts the New Opportunity. He's lost everything and has nowhere else to go. Having lost everything, he's committed to the cause so others don't have to suffer as he has, which means leaving behind that which was familiar.

Tests, Allies, Enemies
Fun & Games
Feeling Disoriented

Once the Change of Plans occurs, the protagonist Crosses the Threshold, moving into a new world with unfamiliar characters, with new rules, with strange behaviors or customs.

This crossover is where the tangible goal and outer motivation are often revealed and where the fun and games begin. These are the moments shown in movie trailers or on movie posters.

The protagonist is meeting characters—allies—from the new world, is tested, and either hears about or meets the enemy for the first time.

During this early experience in the new world, the protagonist will *feel disoriented*. Everything is new — the rules, what's being asked of them, the people, the customs, the landscape, everything. They're being *trained* on how to operate in this new world, and they're *disoriented* as they try to find their place as they're thrown into new situations.

Along the way, the protagonist has help, can ask questions, and receives reasonable answers.

They're learning who is an ally and who isn't and why they aren't.

Pinch Point (37%)
The first glimpse

This first Pinch Point serves as an anchor in the story where the audience gets a *glimpse* of the villainous force headed toward the protagonist.

This Pinch Point is a brief scene from the villain's point of view, revealing their motivation, showing the level of forces or support behind them. We need to see enough to know how much of a danger they are to the protagonist.

Just as we should have seen any skill the protagonist has in Act I, here is where we see the villain's power or skill(s).

The Pinch Point is a scene that reveals what is

unknown to the main character so far—the real danger. This glimpse leads us into the Midpoint.

Act II – Part II

Midpoint Self-Reflection (50%)
Approach to the Innermost Cave / Midpoint
Point of No Return / Mirror Moment
False High / Bridges Burned
Feeling Inauthentic

This plot point is the true middle and starts the second part of Act II.

Also known as the Mirror Moment[3], the protagonist is analyzing not only what they've achieved so far, but what they're facing. They're afraid they're going to fail and fail miserably.

Unfortunately, they can't go back. Bridges have been burned, and they've reached the Point of No Return. They can't return to their prior life; they have no choice but to move forward.

But, they're stuck. They aren't happy with the progress they've made so far. Everything appears to be the same as when they were in the Ordinary World. Only now, it's worse.

This plot point is critical to the story because they

---

[3] Mirror Moment was coined by James Scott Bell, author of *Write Your Novel From the Middle* and other writing how-to books.

realize they *must* change. They're looking in a virtual mirror, seeing their old self, which isn't working. Until this moment, they've been *feeling inauthentic* and feeling it sharply, knowing others see it, too.

If the main character was in pain at the beginning of the story, their pain has increased and is in full measure now. Their emotions are at rock bottom, and they don't like how their wound is still dominating their life. They're recognizing how that wound has affected their decisions until this moment.

The truth of their reality hurts, so they're determined to change.

To succeed, they must go into the unknown and become the person they've always aspired to be.

The question is, do they have the courage, the knowledge, the ability to continue?

This question becomes the thrust into the second part of Act II. This question still feeds into the Key Question. They start figuring out how to make the change.

This is where the audience really begins to root for this main character to succeed. They've seen the character's pain and are feeling it, too. Both the audience and protagonist understand this path forward isn't going to be easy. It looks hard *because it is hard*. But, the protagonist is willing to suck it up and do the work needed, to face the conflict head-on, no longer avoiding it.

And, that emotion has us on the edge of our seat or turning the pages as we continue alongside the protagonist's journey.

The stakes have become higher and the costs are greater than ever.

First Battle
Supreme Ordeal / Bad Guys Close In / Crisis
Feeling Confronted

As the main character moves from their self-realization in the Mirror Moment Midpoint and begins taking steps to become a better person by doing the right thing, they feel determined. But then, the approaching confrontation is made known.

Now, they feel *threatened and confronted*. Their fear increases. The tension rises as danger is ratcheted up. The bad guys are moving in, getting too close for comfort. The lie they've been hiding behind is almost revealed. The truth they're not stepping into is actually working against them, hindering them.

The protagonist prepares for this First Battle or Supreme Ordeal, even if only mentally, emotionally, or psychologically, at this point. The shields go up both physically and mentally. Battle plans get made.

Vogler calls this event a "crisis" because it's not as big as the upcoming climax.

Pinch Point (62%)
The second glimpse

This second Pinch Point again provides a glimpse of the dark force that is approaching. Tensions are high. The villain has no plan to retreat or withdraw. They are determined to win, no matter the cost.

The protagonist wants to react as they've done in the past but can't. They're still struggling to find a way into their new self.

Celebration (False Win)
Seizing the Reward / Break Into 3
Feeling Reborn

The protagonist faces death but will survive this first real skirmish with the enemy, the First Battle. The protagonist is reborn *because of the confrontation*, but it's a false win.

There could have been the appearance of someone dying, and an escape is made. It's a close call, a near death. Yes, they've won, but…. They know there are more battles to come.

For this moment, they're going to focus on the win. They believe they've seized the reward, but have they? Despite the exuberant chatter of the win, the unspoken thought is: can they keep it?

This was a lucky win, and the protagonist is *feeling reborn* and confident in their change, but will it be enough in another battle?

The transition into the new self continues.

Act III

Major Setback Where All is Lost (75%)
The Road Back / Dark Night of the Soul
Feeling Desperate

Then, suddenly, they realize the win wasn't a real win at all. They're stuck. There's no way to move backward or to get out of the way. All they can do is move forward. Their previous feeling of rebirth evaporates.

They want to retreat into past behaviors or go back to what they used to be, but they can't.

This is the final showing of their fear. They're *feeling desperate*.

Climax (90-99%)
Final with 4-Part Finale
Resurrection / Rebirth / Do or Die
Feeling Decisive

Tensions are high. The 4-Part Finale begins.

1. It starts with the gathering of the team where they discuss and come up with a plan. This is their last chance. If the protagonist is acting alone, without a team, they voice their plan to their buddy or mentor aloud, making plans with their new self: *You can do this!*

2. They put the plan into action and get into the enemy's core, the operation headquarters.

3. Once inside, they discover they're trapped. They're surrounded. There's no way out.

4. They readjust their plan and make the ultimate sacrifice of moving forward, even though it will mean their death. In action stories, it could be a physical death. In other stories, it's a psychological death—the death of their reputation, their status, their ranking, even a job, or being ostracized from the community. In a love story, it's the death of a budding relationship. It's a death of their feelings.

The protagonist's arc is completed by the time they've reached the fourth step. They are willing to sacrifice everything to do the right thing.

This *Do or Die* plot point is aptly named. They either *do* it and succeed, or they *die* trying to succeed.

If not a physical death, it's the death of their previous self.

Claiming the Prize
Return Home with the Elixir / Final Image
Feeling Complete

This plot point is the long-awaited resolution.

Because of achieving their arc, becoming the person they've always aspired to be, the protagonist arrives home with the reward of the win or the defeat of the loss, but it feels like a win because they know they did the right thing.

In *feeling complete*, they know they can begin again.

One great example of a loss turned into a win is the story of *Sommersby*, where the hero, deemed a villain by the court's evidence, refuses to tell who he really is for the good of the community.

If the character loses or doesn't achieve their goal, they didn't lose their honor. They're living in their truth now, and that's more important than any loss they suffered.

DIANA STOUT

CHAPTER 10 – THE WORKSHEETS

Tools Required

- standard 3 x 3" inch Post-it notes
- printed 8.5 x 11" versions of the worksheets
- two-fold science board (optional)

The plotting worksheets are designed so that a Post-it note fits inside each square.

If you decide to plot with more than just a basic outline, you can create a portable storyboard, where the plot points are set up as a paradigm on the board. Put as much or as little information on the board to help you plot out the story.

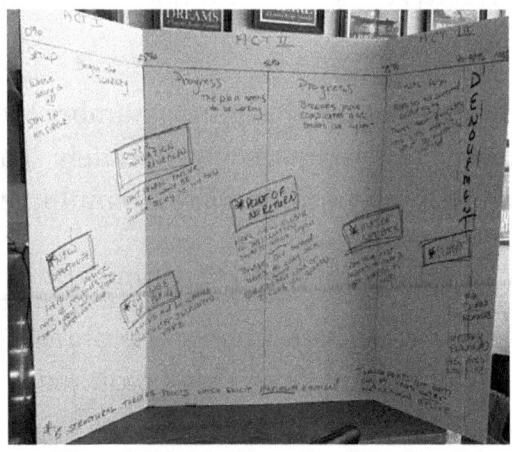

Figure 4: Diana's Science Board Storyboard

I've created a companion *CPE Workbook* that can be purchased. It was designed with full-size worksheets that can be torn out and saved as templates, from which you can scan or copy multiple times.

Or, you can recreate the worksheet pages by following the below directions.

How to Recreate the Worksheets

With any worksheet, you can scan the image, save it as an image, and then INSERT the image into a Word document, enlarging the image as one method.

The character worksheets are easy to replicate by hand as another method.

The plotting worksheets can be replicated by drawing the dividing lines on an 8.5 x 11" piece of paper, as shown on any of the worksheet examples. When drawn correctly, a 3 x 3" Post-it note will fit inside each square.

Make five copies of the sheet, then number the squares or label each square appropriately. Those five pages then become your template for multiple stories.

Post-it Note Directions

When creating your Post-it notes, use phrases, strong active words. Full sentences aren't required. The goal is to visualize the scene in as few words as possible. Less is more at this point.

Once the plot point Post-it notes are in order, you should be able to *read* the story via its core essence.

If there are details you want to record so that you won't forget them, record them on other Post-it notes or on paper elsewhere.

Creating a Bare Bones Outline

At a minimum, you'll want to know the five major plot points that will produce maximum emotional responses.

Once again, these five important plot points are:

1. New Opportunity (10%)
2. Change of Plans (25%)
3. Midpoint Self Reflection (50%)
4. Major Setback Where All is Lost (75%)
5. Climax (90-99%)

The rest of this chapter consists of the plotting worksheets my beta testers used.

While they had directions in their squares because this book hadn't been written yet, those same directions are now provided for you on the page prior to each worksheet.

When creating your own worksheets, you can transfer those directions to the appropriate squares or write your own directions, making the worksheets more useful *for you*.

Plotting Points Post-its #1-6

For all Post-its, use as few words as possible, but which can still provide enough information for you to elaborate with later.

1. Title / Genre / Setting - Record the proposed title, the genre, and starting location. If the story takes place during a specific time period, record that here, too.

2. Key Question - Record the key question being asked and answered by the end of the story.

3. Overall Theme - Record the overall theme in as few words as possible. Like *all that glitters isn't gold*, or *home is where the heart is*, and so forth.

4. Ghost Event or Ghost Person - Name the Ghost Person or Ghost Event, where and when it occurred.

5. Prologue - Record a few words for a prologue scene if a prologue is going to be used.

6. Opening Image - Record a few descriptive words.

CPE

1 - Title / Genre / Setting	2 – Key Question
3 – Overall Theme	4 – Ghost Event or Ghost Person
5 - Prologue	6 – Opening Image

Worksheet 1: Plotting Points 1-6

Plotting Points Post-its #7-12

7. Ordinary World / Current Life – What does the protagonist's current world / life look like?

8. Theme Stated (in dialogue, Throwaway Line) (3%) – Record what comes to mind when you hear the mentor say, *You know what your problem is?* The response should embody the key question.

9. New Opportunity (10%) – What New Opportunity is being offered to the protagonist and by whom? You might want a few words of *why* the opportunity is being offered.

10. Discussion & Decision (Debate) – Record the direction the protagonist chooses initially. If there's a discussion, who is it with? What's the final decision they make?

11. Meeting the Mentor – Who is this person? Where do they meet? A few words about their discussion—the direction the conversation goes.

12. Change of Plans (25%) – What does entering the new world look like?

CPE

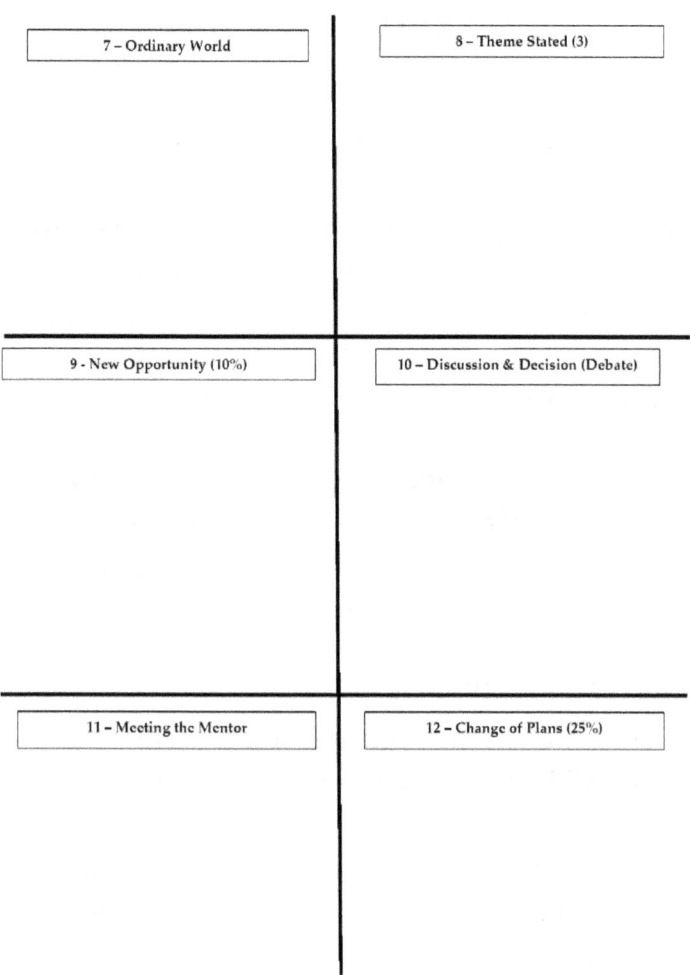

Worksheet 2: Plotting Points 7-12

Plotting Points Post-its #13-18

13. Tests, Allies, Enemies – What are the tests? Who are the allies? Who is the enemy?

14. Pinch Point (37%) – What or who is the dark force the protagonist will face? What is the enemy's goal? What is their world like? This plot point is told from the POV of the enemy, not the protagonist.

15. Midpoint Self-Reflection (50%) – What truth is the protagonist facing about themselves for the first time? How do they feel knowing they can't go back to the original Ordinary World?

16. First Battle – What is the first battle, the confrontation the protagonist faces with the enemy? How does the protagonist win?

17. Pinch Point (62%) – What is the second more dangerous glimpse of the dark force that adds tension to the story? This plot point is told from the POV of the enemy.

18. Celebration (False Win) – What does the celebration of this first battle look like?

CPE

Worksheet 3: Plotting Points 13-18

Plotting Points Post-its #19-24

19. Major Setback (75%) – How does the protagonist appear to lose everything?

20. Climax / Finale (90-99%) – What decision does the protagonist make to resurrect a comeback where they are willing to lose everything else—including their life—because they're now doing the right thing?

21. Part 1, Finale Plan – A few words of the protagonist's plan. Will a team or anyone else be in on the plan?

22. Part 2, Finale Storm – What does the plan's action look like?

23. Part 3, Finale Trapped – What does the trap look like?

24. Part 4, Finale Final Battle – What *do or die* move does the protagonist make to win this battle against all odds?

CPE

19 - Major Setback (75%)

20 – Climax / Finale (90-99%)

21 – Finale Plan

22 – Finale Storm

23 – Finale Trapped

24 – Finale Final Battle

Worksheet 4: Plotting Points 19-24

Plotting Points Post-its #25-30

25. Claiming the Prize – What does the end of this battle look like? What can be claimed as having been won?

26. Final Image – Provide a few words of the final image of the protagonist's feelings as they return home a new person.

The 4 Primary Characters

These last 4 squares feature the 4 primary characters.

Each will have a Post-it with minimum features, which are discussed in detail in the next Character Worksheets section.

27. Protagonist

28. Antagonist

29. Buddy / Mentor / Reflective

30. Love Interest (Fake Antagonist)

CPE

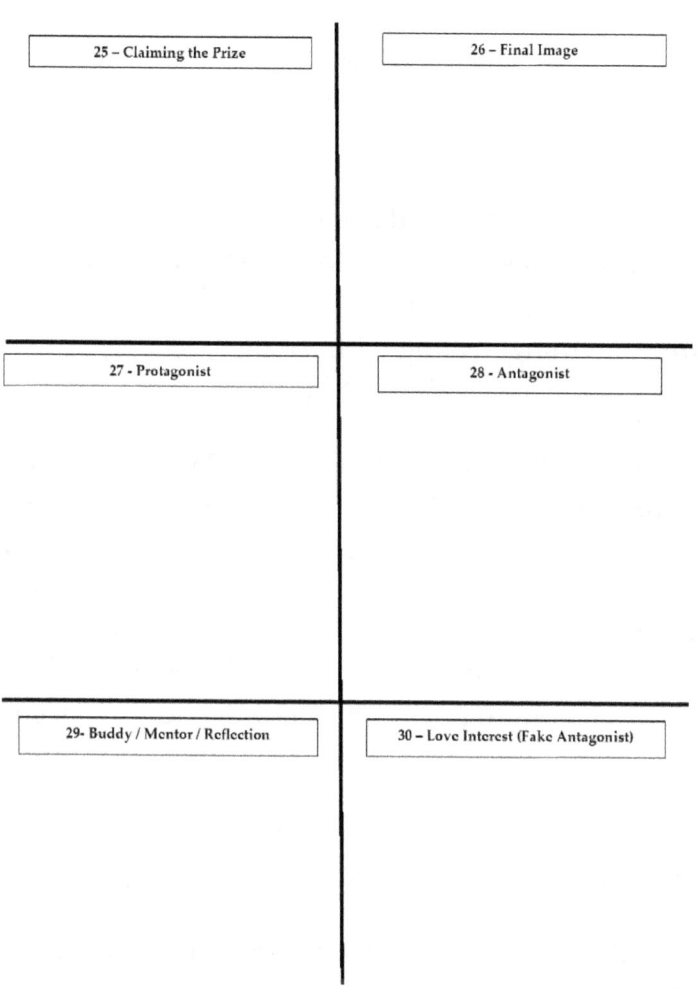

Worksheet 5: Plotting Points 25-30

DIANA STOUT

Character Worksheets

After attending Hauge's workshop and coming home with his Character Worksheet (Figure 6), which became a solid tool for me to use when plotting, I needed something more.

Up until that time, I had been filling out character interview forms that asked for the character's hobbies, habits, likes, dislikes, and what they looked like, but rarely anything dealing with feelings, secrets, or ghosts.

No wonder my characters had been flat, shallow, and resembled paper dolls or talking heads.

Hauge's worksheet gave me a character's goal (want), need, conflict, and wound, but I need a device, a tool that would help me round out the character's traits that turned out to be deeply connected to their need and wound.

So, in 1999, I developed the Character Worksheet, *Putting a Square Peg into a Round World.*

While the other three characters don't need to be as fully developed, the protagonist's worksheet must be filled out completely.

Connecting the other three more deeply to the protagonist's need and wound, thus tied all the characters more fully to the plot.

While we may find a character likable because they rescue kittens, it's their wound that generates our empathy and sympathy for them. Where we want to see them succeed!

Both Hauge's worksheet and my *Putting a Square Peg into a Round World* worksheet helped me further develop my characters more deeply and quickly.

From Michael Hauge's book, *Writing Screenplays That Sell*, used with permission.

	Outer Motivation	Outer Conflict	Inner Motivation	Inner Conflict
Hero				
Nemesis				
Reflection				
Romance				

Worksheet 6: Hauge 1988 motivation & character chart

Putting a Square Peg into a Round World
© Diana Stout, 1999

Name: Name:

[ ]   [ ]

SWOT techniques: Strengths, Weaknesses, Opportunities, and Threats

Strengths	Weaknesses	Strengths	Weaknesses
Opportunities	Threats	Opportunities	Threats

Wound:

Fear:

Lie:

Secret:

Wound Triggers:

Worksheet 7: Putting a Square Peg into a Round World

I use the SWOT (Strengths, Weaknesses, Opportunities, Threats) chart as a brainstorming tool if I struggle to come up with four strong specific traits.

Once I know the character's wound, I list it on this sheet, which helps me fill out the rest of the worksheet regarding their fear, the lie they tell themself based on the wound, the secret surrounding the wound, and their wound triggers.

Because those triggers can feed into their traits, the entire worksheet becomes a brainstorming tool that works alongside Hauge's worksheet.

The following section details how to use these character squares more precisely, and Chapter 11 describes when and how I use this worksheet.

Protagonist Worksheet

Putting a Square Peg into a Round World

Create four character traits: three likeable, and one that is tied solidly to their wound, placing each trait in a corner. At the character's core is their wound.

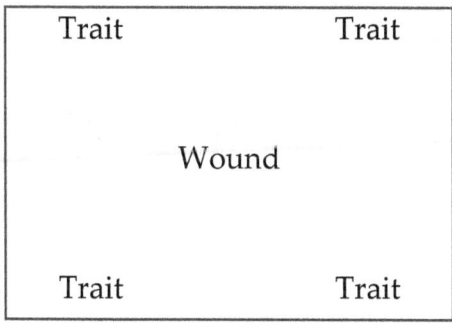

Figure 5: Character Square

Example:

Let's say my protagonist is a nurse. The four traits are *caring, determined, detailed,* and *keeps to herself.* Her wound is that her father died when he became ill and was hospitalized and wasn't treated well—the reason why she became a nurse.

Do you see a problem? I do. This character is dull, especially if I'm writing a thriller, mystery, or horror. We've created a caricature, a cliché of a nurse.

What if we traded *caring* for *revengeful*? If revenge is the real reason she became a nurse, can you see more engaging scene possibilities, a full story with an ending?

For example, she believes a certain doctor murdered her father. She wants him jailed, so she sets out to frame him.

Dialogue will now be filled with subtext. Words coming from a seemingly caring nurse will mean something entirely different when coming from a revengeful nurse.

Can you see how emotion drives a character, which then influences the plot?

(Author's Note: Because this above example is pivotal to creating the main character, the text is duplicated in the *CPE Workbook,* as well.)

CPE

*****

Nemesis / True Villian Worksheet

In *Star Wars,* the development of Darth Vader would equal that of Luke Skywalker. They are adversaries with a long history but unknown to Luke in the beginning. Thus, the glimpses of Vader's world intercut with Luke's journey are important scenes, so this character becomes a large part of story development.

One thing to remember when creating a villain's goal is that every villain believes they're a hero. They want to fix or improve a wrong.

Villains are different though in *how* they achieve their goals, often working against the law or with immoral actions.

*****

Buddy / Reflection / Mentor Worksheet

The focus of this character will be their relationship to the protagonist revealed through dialogue and actions together in the Ordinary World and through Act I.

By the time the story enters Act II, we don't question this relationship at all. They're a team, even if they're at odds with each other.

An example of this relationship at odds was shown in Chapter 6 in *The American President* with the conversation between President Andrew and his Chief of Staff, A.J. MacInerney, who is also his best friend.

*****

Love Interest / (Fake) Antagonist Worksheet

If the story is a romance, this character will be as deeply developed as the protagonist.

This Love Interest character will have a goal of some kind, which is at odds with the protagonist's goal.

More importantly, this character should have as a deep a wound as the protagonist, which echoes in some way the protagonist's wound.

An example of this echo:

In *Safe Haven,* Katie (Julianne Hough) has secretly moved away from her abusive cop husband. Everything she does concerns her ability to stay safe.

Alex (Josh Duhamel) is a widower with two small children, and his goal is to keep his children safe.

See the echo?

Chapter 11 - My Plotting Process

Now that I've shown you the tools I use, let me show you the order of how I use them, providing a tour of my plotting process.

Every project starts with a single idea of either a character or a situation.

Step 1: Writing Character Journals

My first step is to write what I call *character journals*. I'm typing their thoughts, as if they're doing the writing. They get to decide how and where to start.

Usually, they introduce themselves and provide physical attributes like their height, weight, color of hair, eyes, scars from injuries, etc.

Quickly, I hear their voice, their thoughts, and can shapeshift into their bodies, feeling their emotions. Their sentences become flavored with that voice, their way of talking, word choice, things they observe.

They tell me about their parents, their problems, what it was like in school, jobs they've had, dreams and desires.

Anytime they gloss over a problem or something in

the past, I'll ask questions of:

> *How did that feel?*
> *What did you do then?*

In asking questions, I'm digging down with a goal to uncover their wound.

Eventually, I can hear a change in their voice, and that's where I really drill down, asking questions. Sure enough, the wound is there and revealed, but with a promise I won't tell anyone else.

I always promise.

And then, they reveal their wound, talking about how it happened, how old they were, who else was involved. Everything. For now, it's our secret.

It can take a day to write just one journal, several days to record two or more.

Once the characters and I are done with the journals, and where I've made Post-it notes with possible scenes where I could use any of the information they shared, I let that pile of Post-its rest for now.

These Post-its contain wounds, triggers, conversation topics, anything big or small that can be incorporated into the story.

The first time I wrote two character journals for a romance novel involving a hero and heroine, I had my teenage daughter read them. Each journal was typed and about 3-4 pages long, single-spaced.

When she finished reading them, she looked at me and asked, "Who wrote these?"

"I did."

"No, who wrote these?"

"I did."

"No," she said, slowly and with emphasis, "*Who* wrote these? They're from two different people, other people, not you. This isn't your writing."

I grinned.

When I explained I was merely the typist for two characters, her eyes widened. "That's crazy."

Her reaction was perfect. My characters were real.

Step 2: Filling in the Character Squares

The journals finished, I fill in the character worksheets and create the character squares.

I'm adding to the stack of Post-it notes anything that can add depth to the plot, characters, or emotion.

While I know from experience that I may not use all of the Post-it notes, at least I have them should I need them. Far better to write them down and not use them than to not record my ideas and later wish I had.

*****

To show you how the Character Squares and Hauge's Character Chart work, I'm sharing the worksheets to my family Christmas story, set in the Deep South, *Charlie's Christmas Carole*.

Readers would tell me, *This reads like a TV movie!*

It's one-line blurb:

> When middle school principal Charlie Dickens must eliminate the Christmas pageant or lose his new job, he struggles with his daughter who just won the lead, the play's director—his childhood sweetheart, and a magical reindeer he saw as a boy.

The story is a screenplay I wrote in 1996. It was a quarterfinalist in the Austin Heart of Films contest, a semi-finalist in the Writer's Network contest, and had been optioned with a producer, who wanted to option it a second time, which I rejected.

Today, it's published in script format as an eBook through Amazon's Kindle Unlimited and as a print book from any bookstore, including Amazon.

Here are the two Character Squares for Charlie and Carole. Charlie is the protagonist and Carole is the Romance / Fake Antagonist character.

CPE

Charlie's Christmas Carole

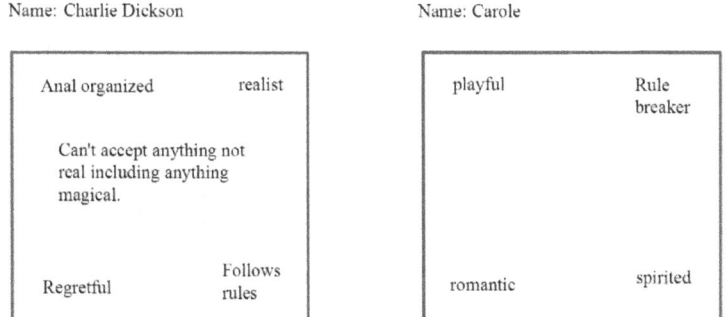

Figure 6: CCC character squares

Carole has no wound. She believes in magic. Both Carole and Charlie each have a daughter who both believe in magic like Carole. The same age and in the same class, the two girls become best friends.

The story starts when as young children living in South Georgia, Carole and Charlie are best friends. One winter day, they see a reindeer. It begins snowing. They look up and when they look back at the reindeer, it's gone. Shortly afterward, Charlie and his mother are forced to move away.

I *saw* the above scene as I was filling out squares. Quickly, I wrote the scene out, recording everything, then put that scene aside.

*****

Once I believe the journals are done and the Character Square worksheets are filled out as much as possible,

I move to Step #3.

If I do have any blanks on the Character Square Worksheet, I'll work back and forth between it and the Character Chart in this next step until I'm satisfied.

Step 3: Filling in Hauge's Character Chart

While this chart characterizes the titles that Hauge uses in his book and used in the workshop, the Hero—the protagonist—can be any sex and any age.

The Hero's Inner Conflict square is the most important square because all the other characters are tied to this wound. So, it's the first cell that I fill, and it comes from my character square.

For the other characters, I fill in their Outer Motivation as it ties to the Hero's wound and fill in the Nemesis' Outer Conflict as it should oppose the Hero's Outer Motivation.

As you can see in Figure 7, not all of the cells are filled out. They didn't need to be. Genre will dictate which cells of the other primary characters need to be filled.

Continuing the story of *Charlie's Christmas Carole*: Years later, Charlie—a widower—returns to the town of his youth and reconnects with Carole, but he's not the same person she once knew.

Charlie's Christmas Carole

	Outer Motivation	Outer Conflict	Inner Motivation	Inner Conflict
Hero Charlie	To follow the rules – to be a good principal	Carole	To do what's right	Can't accept unreality
Nemesis School Board	Wants budget cut; Charlie must eliminate school pageant	Charlie is stalling		
Reflection Lindsey (his daughter)	She wants to find a mom	Dad resists her antics		
Romance Carole	Pageant director, she wants to keep her job	Charlie & school board	To find love with Charlie	

Figure 7: Hauge's Character Chart for CCC

Notice how Charlie's wound is affected by each of the others' Outer Motivations.

Charlie never recovered from the pain-filled early life when his father left the family, forcing him and his mother to move. As a result, he lost the ability to believe in magic. Now, he can't accept anything not real. Christmas had been his late wife's holiday, not his. Adding to his childhood wound, his wife has died; he lost his last job because he didn't follow the rules, and now he's confronted with all of that pain again, both in his personal life and with his job.

*****

Once I start filling in the Character Chart, I go back and forth among these first three steps, adding and refining as needed.

By using these three tools together—the Journals, Square, and Chart—I'm creating characters with depth.

I stop once I've determined that I can't add anything more.

Once upon a time, I used to spend hours filling out interview forms of likes, dislikes, hobbies, foods they ate, their eye and hair color, height, education, friends while growing up, and so forth.

Discovering the wound is my primary focus of discovery. Everything else is secondary. Letting them reveal these things in their Journal becomes organic.

As I work their journals and then the worksheets, the characters come to life and appear in my mind's eye. I can hear them and they're telling me everything what I *need* to know about them.

Step 4: Creating Post-its

Simultaneously, as I work through the previous three steps, I'm collecting Post-it notes. It's important to grow the collection—with fears, flaws, triggers, memories good and bad, comments, and actions—anything that can be used in a scene. Anything and everything.

I never worry whether I have too many or too few

Post-its. No judgements or standards are allowed here. Even though this collecting of Post-it notes is listed as its own step, it's actually a part of the first three steps, too. Only after I think I can't add another Post-it note to the pile, do I move to step 5.

Step 5: Identifying the 5 Key Plot Points

With my printed plotting worksheets spread out in front of me, I sort the Post-its, placing the layering techniques to the side for the moment: the symbols, subplots, and anything not related to the protagonist.

Any scene related to the villain gets put into its own pile.

I'm looking for five scenes that pertain to the protagonist; and in particular, those scenes that have them butting up against their wound that will escalate danger and maximize feelings.

I'm looking to set in place these five major plot points first:

- New Opportunity (10%)
- Change of Plans (25%)
- Midpoint, Self-Reflection (50%)
- Major Setback Where All is Lost (75%)
- Claiming the Prize (99-100%)

We tend to not hurt our characters, but that's exactly what needs to happen as the story moves past the Midpoint and moves into the second part of Act II.

When coaching writers who are lost in their story, I collaborate with them to expose this bare-bones plot first. It's the story's spine.

Once they find and set these five plot points in place, suddenly, they see how emotion and rising tension were lacking. They weren't hurting their characters enough in the stories. Additionally, they had one or more of the five major plot points in the wrong place.

Step 6: Organizing Scenes

Once the five key plot points are in position, now it becomes an easier job to place the rest of the Post-it notes on the plotting pages.

This is where plot holes stand out like the black holes that they are. What am I missing? Do I need more glimpses of the dark forces in their world? Do I need more interaction between characters? Is every scene showing character, emotion, or moving the plot forward?

Here's a photo (Figure 8) of what my first-draft early plotting looks like when I used mini 1.5 x 2" Post-it notes and a file folder divided into three acts for my novelette, *Harbor House: Say You Will,* a romance, historical Gothic, which was published in a January 2024 anthology, *Unlock My Heart.*

Because *Harbor House: Say You Will* was only 11,000 words, the number of scene needs are fewer than those needed as shown in Figure 9 on the next page, which represents *Harbor House: Last Blood*, a continuation of the story 100 years later as a psychological thriller. It's planned as an October 2024 release. For this book, I needed to use the larger two-fold science board as my storyboard along with multi-colored Post-it notes.

Harbor House: Say You Will is exampled in the plotting sheets in Chapter 12, where I show you how these Post-it notes are used on the plotting sheets.

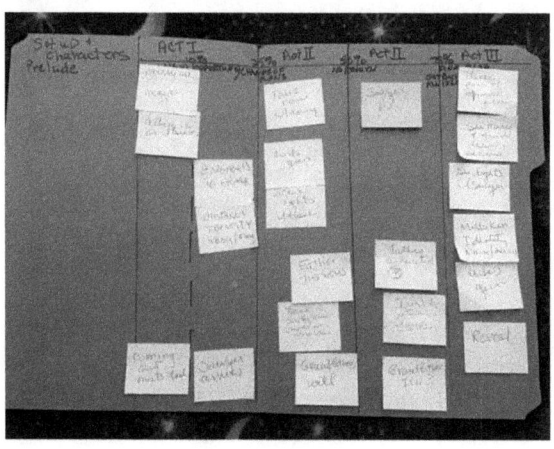

Figure 8: File Folder Plotting

Immediately, by looking at the story as a whole, I can ask the following questions, and I don't stop tweaking these Post-its either in content (adding, removing) or by moving them around until I can answer the questions satisfactorily.

- Am I starting the story on the day that isn't the same as every other day?
- Do I have the 5 most important plot points in the right places? Meaning: does the tension rachet up and up and up, continually rising toward the climax?
- Am I able to find the key question by looking at the character's tangible goal, which also addresses their wound and how the story ends?

Figure 9: Science Board as Storyboard

Step 7: Starting the Story

Once I believe the plotting is done, where I've layered in emotion and characterization, I type it all, plugging everything into one document outline that resembles a synopsis or script treatment with scene headings and paragraphs for every scene.

I provide the template of my Outline Document in the *CPE Workbook*.

Each scene heading—called a slugline in scripts—contains pertinent information: location, time of day, and a word or two about what happens.

Examples:

- Backyard, protagonist home, dusk, wound triggered.
- Inside garage, backseat of car, midnight, searching for necklace.
- Store mall, food court, noon, meets father.

When I was developing my romance series of 7 couples and their stories all taking place over the same 15 days, my headers identified the day, location, who the scene involved if needed, and a word of action.

- Day 1 – morning, Clint's garage, meets mechanic
- Day 5 – just before sunset, picnic at lake
- Day 10 – diner, Cutter, Clint, Joe, and Mason, discussing party

Each scene heading is then put into Word's Table of Contents by clicking on *References, Add Text*, and choosing a level. Anything typed under that heading belongs with that heading.

Once the heading has been referenced, now I can use the Navigation tool, which is located under *View*, and clicking the *Navigation Pane*, which opens the Pane to the left of my document, showing me the Table of Contents.

If a scene needs to be moved, I can grab the scene with my cursor and slide it to a new location, which moves all of the header's contents, too.

Once everything is typed and includes the Table of Contents at the beginning of the document, which will be included in the final manuscript, I have a document of 10–60 pages.

I go to the first plot element and under that header, I start writing the story's first draft.

For now, all the scene headings stay, but any text originally written and placed in the outline gets morphed into the book, so the book grows as I move from scene to scene. The pantsering comes alive through character voice in dialogue, reactions, and introspection.

My paragraph outline guides me from scene to scene, as I pantser through the story, easily and smoothly.

Should I come across a scene that I'm not sure what to write, I skip it for now.

I want to write the first draft quickly, so I write the

scenes I'm already seeing on the movie screen in my head.

Step 8: Editing

It's in the second draft that I go back and start working on those scenes I previously had skipped. Usually, they're easier to write now that I've written the ending.

As I go through the many drafts of editing, should I have to move any scene, because of the scene headings and the Navigation tool, I can easily make the change, and then bridge the paragraph(s) appropriately into their new location.

Once I'm assured the book's organization is correct, that's when I remove the scene headings, converting them into chapter headings, deleting those within the chapters that are no longer needed. Usually, instead, those become scene breaks.

Chapter 12 – FAQ, Part II

You mentioned plot points and genres earlier. How do these plot points affect different genres?

Most all writing—fiction and nonfiction alike—are formulaic per a genre's structure.

It's true for a children's storybook, query letters, thesis papers, short stories, and fiction: mysteries, science fiction, general literature, romances, horror, and so forth. There are exceptions but not many.

I became aware of these structured plot points as discussed by screenwriters, story consultants, and those associated with screenplays and film.

I learned that movie scripts were either high concept or soft stories. High concept will have lots of action, chase scenes, deal with science fiction, larger-than-life situations. There's lots of sub-text.

Soft stories are romances, the Christmas romance movies produced by TV networks. Other soft stories are often character driven rather than plot driven. Soft stories have *lots* of dialogue. Lots of feelings being discussed and worked through.

That's not to say that a character driven movie can't be high concept because they can. It just depends on the goal, the action within the movie.

When I started applying these plot points to my fiction, which was romance writing, I noticed some plot points were less developed than others.

Regardless, though, of whether you're writing a soft story or a high-concept story, each will fully engage the five main plot points that Hauge proclaims are points where "elicit maximum emotion" should occur. These are the plot points that keep us as readers and viewers engaged.

*****

Remember my file folder storyboard with mini Post-it notes in Step #6 in the last chapter? Here is where I show you what the Plotting Worksheets would look like if those Post-it notes were on the worksheets.

As you review them, you may question why some plot points are blank. For this story, I didn't need to fill them in. How come, you ask?

First, this story is a romance. The Key Question is pretty standard for all romances: Will the hero and heroine work out their differences so that they can love one another unencumbered by those differences?

For a number of mysteries, the key question becomes: Will the (police, amateur detective, etc.) solve the crime? Or, can the protagonist find the killer before they become a victim, too?

Your genre *and* your particular story will determine the Key Question.

Regarding the Ghost Event or Ghost Person – For this story, there isn't one, other than what occurs in the prologue.

You'll notice, too that I don't have an Antagonist or Love Interest named. With this first draft, I was still determining who was who. That's where pantsering the scenes as I started writing determined who those people would be.

Yes, I knew the ending, but I wasn't sure in this early plotting, *which* person would be the true Love Interest.

And so forth.

Second, did you notice how there are just a few words or a phrase for each plot point?

I already knew the scene(s) behind those words. In a document, I fully wrote out the details, so I won't forget them, and they became part of the outline synopsis, from which I wrote my first draft.

These worksheets are the equivalent of a first draft in developing the plot. Because I had so many blank worksheet cells, I went back to the journals and dug deeper, questioning more events, and broadening their traits.

That's when I discovered a couple of the characters had been hiding feelings and events. That activity had me adding Post-its to the plotting worksheets before I started typing everything.

Again, your process can be entirely different from mine!

Use these worksheets so that they best suit *your needs*!

Do what works for you!

May your writing journey become even more successful, and you're able to more firmly nail down a process that works *for you*!

Happy plotting and happy writing!

DIANA STOUT

Harbor House: Say You Will
Plotting Point Worksheets

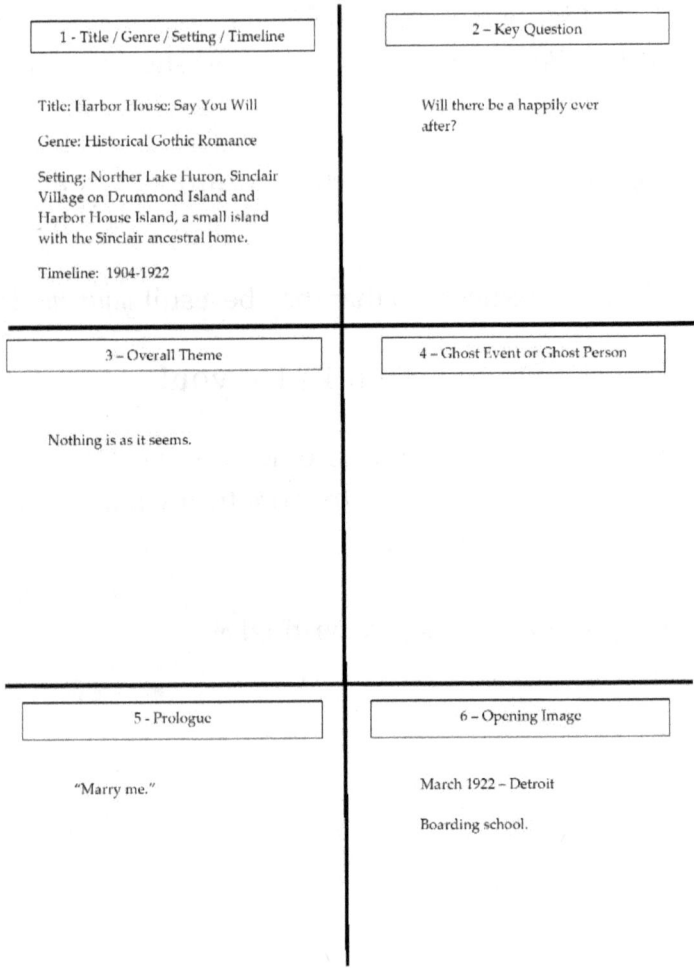

1 - Title / Genre / Setting / Timeline	2 – Key Question
Title: Harbor House: Say You Will Genre: Historical Gothic Romance Setting: Norther Lake Huron, Sinclair Village on Drummond Island and Harbor House Island, a small island with the Sinclair ancestral home. Timeline: 1904-1922	Will there be a happily ever after?
3 – Overall Theme	4 – Ghost Event or Ghost Person
Nothing is as it seems.	
5 - Prologue	6 – Opening Image
"Marry me."	March 1922 – Detroit Boarding school.

Figure 10: Diana's Plotting Points 1-6

CPE

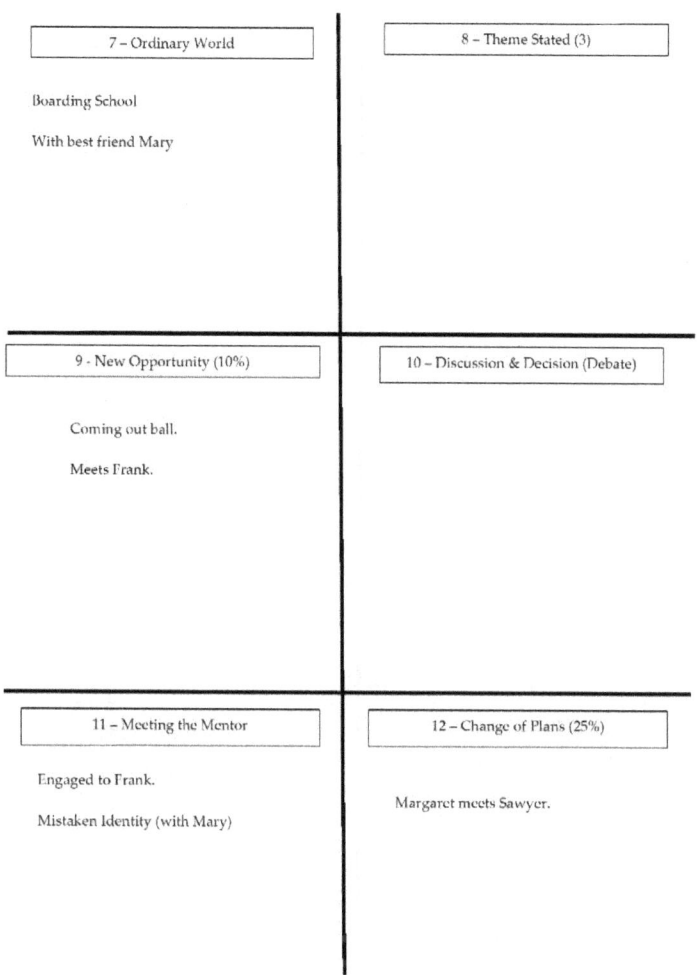

Figure 11: Diana's Plotting Points 7-12

DIANA STOUT

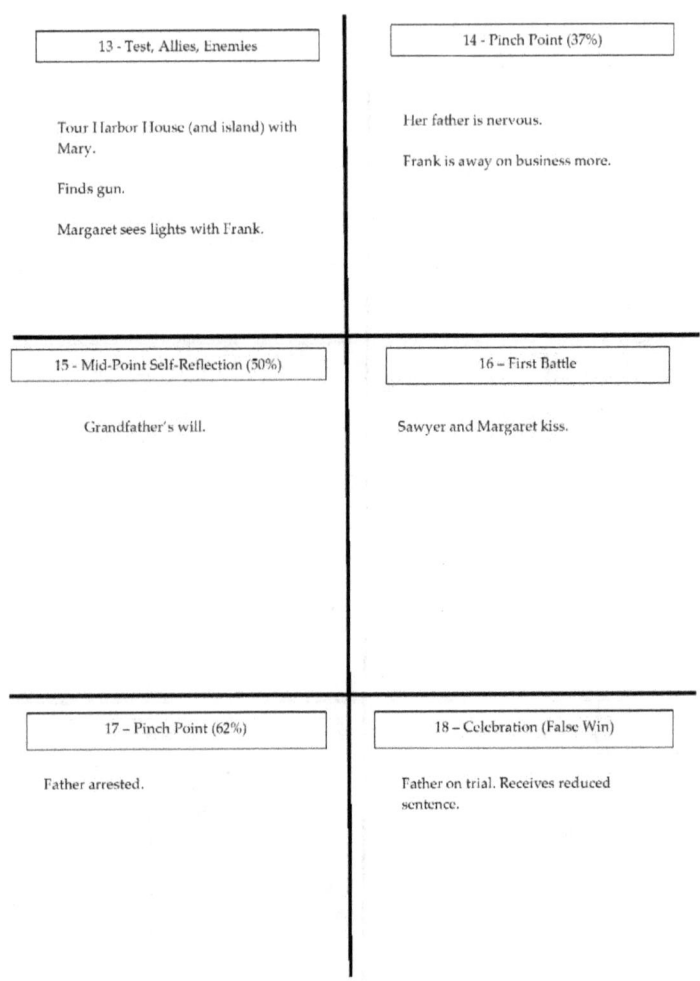

Figure 12: Diana's Plotting Points 13-18

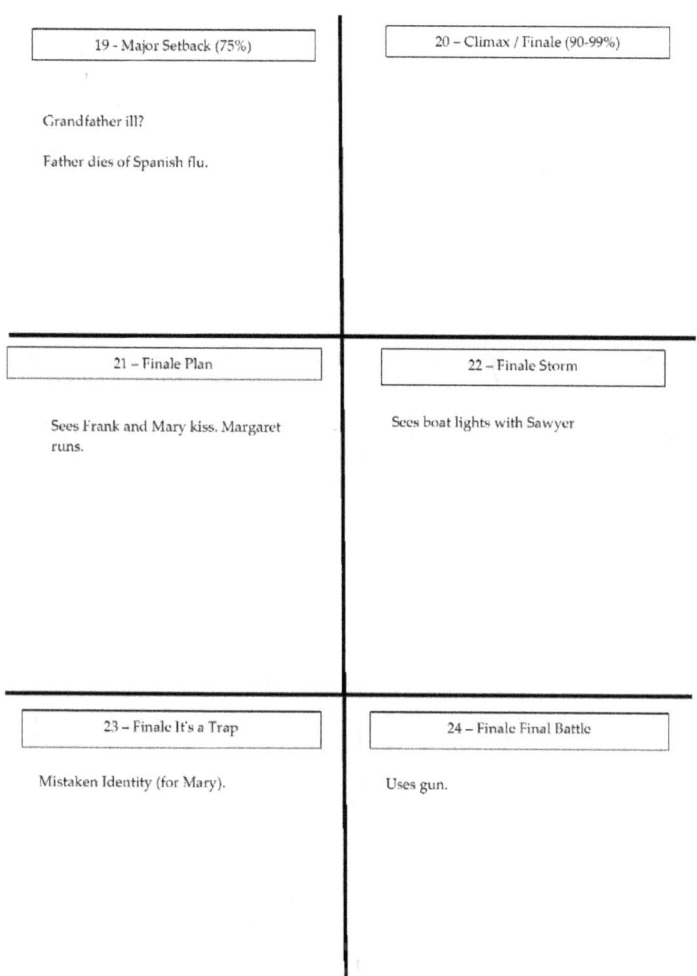

Figure 13: Diana's Plotting Points 19-24

25 – Claiming the Prize	26 – Final Image
Reveal.	

27 - Protagonist	28 - Antagonist
Margaret Sinclair (heroine)	

29- Buddy / Mentor / Reflection	30 – Love Interest (Fake Antagonist)
Mary	

Figure 14: Diana's Plotting Points 25-30

Recommended Reading

The Anatomy of Genres, John Truby
The Anatomy of Story: 22 Steps to Becoming a Master Storyteller, John Truby
Creating Unforgettable Characters, Linda Seger
The Hero's 2 Journey, Michael Hauge & Christopher Vogler (DVD)
How to Write a Novel Using the Snowflake Method, Randy Ingermanson
Poetics, Aristotle
The Power of Myth, Joseph Campbell
Save the Cat! (on screenwriting), Sydney Blake
Save the Cat! Writes a Novel, Jessica Brody
Screenplay, Syd Field
Storytelling Made Easy, Michael Hauge
Techniques of the Selling Writer, Dwight V. Swain
Write Your Novel From the Middle, James Scott Bell
The Writer's Journey, Christopher Vogler
Writing Screenplays that Sell, Michael Hauge
Writing for Story, Jon Franklin
Your Storytelling Potential, Mitchell German

ARTICLES

"A New Character-Driven Hero's Journey," *Cracking Yarns*. Allen Palmer, April 4, 2021.
http://www.crackingyarns.com.au/2011/04/04/a-new-character-driven-heros-journey-2/

"The Five-Step Finale," *Save the Cat!* Blake Snyder. December 17, 2007. https://savethecat.com/tips-and-tactics/the-five-step-finale

About the Author

Diana Stout, MFA, Ph.D. is an award-winning writer, who taught writing classes for a decade online, then returned to school as a nontraditional student, so she could combine her two passions of teaching and writing and become an accredited English professor, teaching writing classes in college classrooms. Her students would tell her, "You smile when you talk about writing."

"A writer to watch. "She's a screenwriter, author, editor, and writing coach. She's been published across the genres, in multiple media, both traditionally and as an indie publisher through her company, Sharpened Pencils Productions LLC.

Today, she writes full time. Her greatest joy after publishing her books of fiction, nonfiction, and screenplays is helping other writers. She achieves this through her how-to books, teaching classes, and as a speaker to writing groups.

When not writing, she enjoys movies, reading, and jigsaw puzzles.

Also by Diana Stout

Nonfiction
Finding Your Fire & Keeping It Hot
The Super Simple Easy Basic Cookbook

Epic Fantasy
Grendel's Mother

Romance
Determined Hearts
Love's New Beginnings
Tomorrow's Wish for Love

Laurel Ridge Novella Series
Laurel Ridge: Seven Ways to Love
Shattered Dreams #1
Burning Desire #2
Arrested Pleasures #3
Buried Hearts #4
Tangled Passions #5
Reserved Yearnings #6
Sweet Cravings #7

Literary / Short Story
Maggie's Story

Anthology / Collections
Lost and Found (story contribution & editor)
Unlock My Heart (story contribution)

Screenplays published as books
David & Goliath
Charlie's Christmas Carole

Follow Diana Stout

You can follow links to her social media from her website, Sharpened Pencils Productions:

sharpenedpencilsproductions.com

Blogs

Behind the Scenes – life as a writer, dianastout.net

Into the Core – life as an intuitive, dianastout.com

Featured Guests with Diana Stout, dianastout.org

Can You Help?

I hope you have found this plotting workbook helpful. Please consider leaving a review.

Reviews can be short, such as:
- I loved this book!
- I liked this book and found it helpful.

It's not the length of a review that counts; it's the number of reviews that a book receives that engage the algorithms so that the site advertises a book more often.

THANK YOU!

You can leave the same review at multiple locations, such as BookBub.com, Goodreads.com, and Amazon.com.

I am most appreciative of your support!

www.ingramcontent.com/pod-product-compliance
Lightning Source LLC
Chambersburg PA
CBHW060759050426
42449CB00008B/1455